A PRACTICAL GUIDE TO
EXOTIC
PETS

Spotted turtle *(Clemmys guttata)*

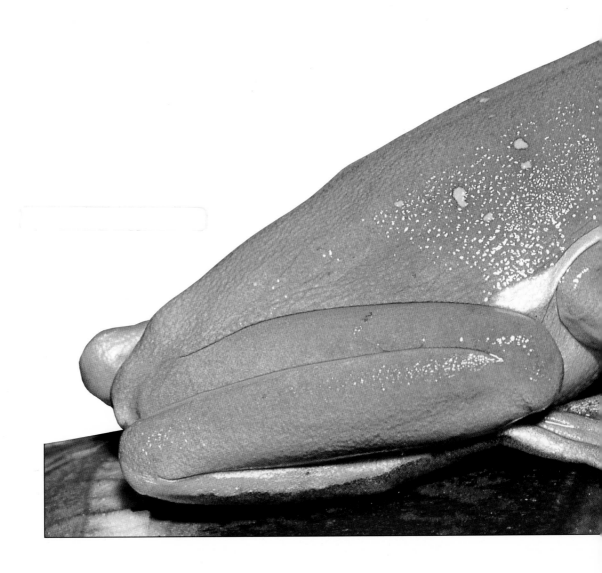

American green treefrog (*Hyla cinerea*)

A PRACTICAL GUIDE TO

EXOTIC
PETS

CHRIS MATTISON

CLB

3368 A Practical Guide to Exotic Pets
This edition published in 1999 by CLB
an imprint of Quadrillion Publishing Ltd
Godalming, Surrey, GU7 1XW, UK

Distributed in the USA by
Quadrillion Publishing, Inc.
230 Fifth Avenue, New York 10001

ISBN 1-84100-244-5
Printed in Hong Kong

Edited and designed: Ideas into Print
Species photography: Chris Mattison
Studio photography: Neil Sutherland
Typesetting: Ideas into Print and Ash Setting and Printing
Production: Ruth Arthur, Sally Connolly, Neil Randles
Director of Production: Gerald Hughes
Color separations: Advance Laser Graphic Arts (International) Ltd.

THE AUTHOR

Chris Mattison is a writer based in Yorkshire, England. He has a degree in zoology and specializes in reptiles, amphibians and other unusual animals. These interests have taken him to southern Europe, North and South America, and Southeast Asia, and he has given lectures in North America and several European countries. He has written and illustrated eight previous books and his photographs have appeared in a number of natural history and travel magazines. This book features 120 of his photographs.

STUDIO PHOTOGRAPHER

Neil Sutherland has more than 25 years experience in a wide range of photographic fields, including still-life, portraiture, reportage, natural history, cookery, landscape and travel. His work has been published in countless books and magazines throughout the world.

Left: Striped day gecko.   ***Endpapers:*** *Albino ("Golden") Burmese python.*

CONTENTS

Right: The Everglades ratsnake, Elaphe obsoleta rossalleni, *comes from Florida. Like many other snakes, it will make a good pet and live for many years, as long as it is given the correct living conditions.*

Keeping exotic pets

Exotic pets can be divided into three broad categories: invertebrates, amphibians, and reptiles. Although they differ from each other in many ways, they do have some features in common. To begin with, they are all ectotherms. This means that they are unable to generate heat from within and cannot raise their body temperatures above those of their surroundings in the same way as mammals and birds. Different methods of providing this extra heat are described later, but the important message is that heat is an essential requirement. These animals do not just dislike being cold - they cannot function when they are cold and will eventually die. Remember, too, that insects, arachnids, amphibians, and reptiles all shed, or molt, their skin as they grow and are especially vulnerable to damage at this time.

None of the animals discussed in this book are "pets" in the true sense of the word, i.e. they are not domesticated and cannot be expected to respond to their owner in the same way as a dog or parrot, for instance. In addition, because of their background, they tend to be shy. In nature, they avoid their many enemies by hiding or by adopting cryptic coloration and postures; if they are forced out into the open in a bare or inadequately furnished cage, they may become stressed. By providing hiding places, you will help them to feel more secure and they will gradually gain enough confidence to behave normally. Whenever possible - and especially if you are a beginner - try to select cultured or captive-bred specimens, as they will adapt more easily. In any case, there are restrictions on the import of certain species from the wild because they are becoming over-exploited. Finally, before buying any pets at all, make sure that you will be able to obtain all the food and equipment you will need, some of which is rather specialized.

Right: The eastern tiger swallowtail butterfly, Papilio glaucus, is one of many large and showy North American species that can be raised in captivity and then released into a suitable habitat. Only release species if they are found locally.

Left: This hatchling gold-dust day gecko, Phelsuma laticauda, has just struggled out of its egg. Like all reptiles, it is completely independent of its parents as soon as it hatches and is well able to fend for itself.

Right: The milky eyes and muted coloration of this Central American ratsnake, Elaphe flavirufa, are indications that it is preparing to shed, or molt, its skin. In a few days, the eyes will clear and then, about four days later, the snake will crawl out of its old skin. Snakes often lose their appetite immediately before shedding.

Right: The Riobamba marsupial frog, Gastrotheca riobambae, is a typical tree frog with sticky toes and large eyes. It has remarkable breeding habits, however, because the female carries her eggs in a pouch in her back until they hatch into tadpoles. Overall, frogs and toads have a wider variety of reproductive methods than most other groups of animals.

Handling exotic pets

Many people who would otherwise enjoy keeping exotic pets are put off by the thought of handling the animals. In fact, many exotic pets can be kept indefinitely without any direct handling and, indeed, this is the best arrangement for many species, as they are easily stressed if they are disturbed and handled excessively.

Other people like to have occasional physical contact with their pets and although this can lead to problems with certain species, many others can be carefully handled without harming either the keeper or the animal. As a rule, do not allow young children to handle exotic pets.

Left: You can usually pick up terrestrial frogs, toads, and salamanders without too much trouble, but handle them carefully, as most species are delicate. Do not handle them more than is necessary. Some salamanders and frogs, notably the poison dart frogs, fire-bellied toads, and the European fire salamander (as shown here), secrete poisonous substances from glands in their skin. These substances are only dangerous if swallowed. Always wash your hands thoroughly after handling these creatures.

Left: Small lizards, such as this fat-tailed gecko, can be encouraged to climb onto your hand, but make sure they do not leap off halfway through the operation! Do not grab small lizards by the tail - it may come away in your hand. Grasp large lizards such as monitors, firmly around the neck with one hand and support the body with the other. With very large specimens, you may need to trap the tail under one arm to prevent it thrashing about.

Left: The only safe way to handle scorpions is with a pair of long forceps. To avoid damaging the scorpion, it is a good idea to cover the tips of the forceps with small pads of foam rubber.

Below: Most snakes can be picked up and held firmly but gently around the middle of the body. Even non-venomous snakes can give a painful bite. If they are tame, grasp them firmly behind the head while supporting the body with the other hand. It is sometimes possible to lift aggressive snakes out of their cage using a "snake-hook." Remember that all large snakes are potentially dangerous. Do not handle them unnecessarily, do not carry them wrapped around your neck and do not give them to children to handle.

Left: Do not handle large spiders at all. Many can give a painful bite and others are easily damaged. The best way to move them is to allow them to crawl into a tub or box and replace the lid.

Below: The best way to handle species such as stick insects (a jungle nymph is featured here), caterpillars, and mantids is to allow them to climb onto your hand. Moths can also be handled in this way, but are easier to cope with during the day when they are less active. (If they are day-flying species, then handle them in the evening.) Pick up crickets and locusts between the finger and thumb. If you can catch hold of their hindlegs at the same time, they will be easier to control. Insects to be offered as food can be slowed down by placing them in a refrigerator for a few minutes.

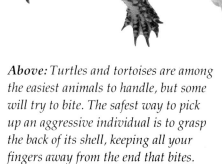

Above: Turtles and tortoises are among the easiest animals to handle, but some will try to bite. The safest way to pick up an aggressive individual is to grasp the back of its shell, keeping all your fingers away from the end that bites.

Below: Very few frogs or toads bite, but large bullfrogs may try. Hold them firmly around their back legs (as here), but do not handle them unnecessarily. Use an aquarium net to catch and move aquatic species of amphibians.

KEEPING INVERTEBRATES

Invertebrates are animals without backbones. The most likely subjects to be kept in captivity are various sorts of insects, including stick insects and moths, arachnids (spiders and scorpions), myriapods (millipedes), mollusks (snails), and crustaceans (crabs and related animals).

Keeping invertebrates can provide an insight into the lives of these fascinating and often beautiful animals. Many of them reproduce under fairly simple conditions and you can follow the whole life cycle in the comfort of your own home. There are two basic life cycles among the insects. The lives of some, such as butterflies and moths, are divided into several stages, known as the larva (a caterpillar, for example), the pupa, or chrysalis, and the adult, or imago. Other insects hatch from their eggs as tiny replicas of their parents and they are called nymphs. Nymphs go through a number of molts until they reach full size. In species in which the adults have wings, the nymphs lack these, but small wing "buds" become progressively more obvious each time they molt. The stages between molts are called "instars" so, for instance, crickets and locusts go through five to eight instars before they are adult. Only the adults are capable of breeding. The life cycles of invertebrates other than insects tend to follow the latter pattern.

Some invertebrates are easier to look after than others, but even inexperienced keepers should be able to maintain a small selection of animals. The following pages give practical advice on the general care and maintenance of invertebrates. This is followed by descriptions of some of the species of interest, together with more detailed information on keeping and rearing them.

Housing invertebrates

Before acquiring any animals, it is important to consider their housing requirements and to make sure that the necessary food and equipment are readily available. Because invertebrates come in many shapes and sizes, it follows that they can be housed in a wide range of cages. Some of the basic designs are described here, but a few modifications may be necessary to make them suitable for certain groups of species.

Perhaps the most useful design is a tall, transparent container with ventilation holes in the top. In its simplest form this can be a glass jar with a nylon mesh top held in place with a rubber band. Cages sold specifically for housing small insects, including caterpillars, are based on this simple design but come in a variety of sizes. An

Below: *This cylindrical cage made of transparent plastic, with a metal or plastic base and a ventilated lid, is intended for caterpillars. It provides plenty of height - essential for molting.*

Right: *A mesh cage is useful for rearing caterpillars or stick insects outdoors. It can be suspended from a hook or branch. As it dries out rather quickly, remember to spray the contents frequently.*

alternative design, useful for stick insects and mantids, etc., consists of a wooden frame covered with nylon mesh. The front of the cage is removable, allowing you to replace food and clean out the interior. The amount of ventilation can be controlled by fixing clear plastic over one or more of the sides. A variation on this design consists of a cylindrical mesh cage that can be hung from a hook or converted to a free-standing cage by placing thin wooden struts between the upper and lower frame. This type of cage is particularly useful for housing insects that are seasonal, especially caterpillars; when not in use it

Right: Small plastic aquariums are cheap, strong, and light and have well-fitting lids, very important with certain types of "pets"! This one is standing on a low-output heat mat to provide a little extra warmth for a tropical scorpion.

Below: Plastic plant propagators, transparent food containers, etc., can be adapted for housing invertebrates, either temporarily or permanently. They are readily available, cheap to buy, and easy to store when not in use.

can be collapsed and stored away easily. Plant propagators of varying sizes and plastic food containers are also useful for animals that are only going to be housed temporarily.

A glass or plastic aquarium is more suitable for spiders, scorpions, snails, hermit crabs, and millipedes. Several ranges of these cages are available commercially, including some designed specifically for invertebrates and other small pets. It is essential that the lid fits well.

Cage furnishings

What goes inside the cage, along with the invertebrates, depends partly on what they require and partly on what you would like to see. The priority should always be to provide a suitable habitat for the animals and aesthetic considerations should come second to this.

You will nearly always need to cover the floor of the cage with a suitable substrate. Although this varies from species to species, a fairly small selection of substrate types should cover most requirements. Sand and aquarium gravel are readily available and

suitable for many species. Their main drawback is the difficulty of cleaning them, but small quantities can be discarded and replaced without excessive expense. Bark chippings are more appropriate for forest-floor invertebrates and for species that climb. Use the finest grade, sometimes known as "orchid bark." This material will retain moisture without becoming waterlogged after it has been sprayed, which helps to create a humid environment. Less attractive, but possibly more hygienic, are paper kitchen towels, which are easily replaced when soiled. For display purposes, dead leaves or bracken provide an attractive and natural substrate. For invertebrates that mimic plants, such as leaf and stick insects, it is worth making an attempt to use leaves and twigs that match the animals.

Other furnishings are largely a matter of taste, but avoid creating too many nooks and crannies that may harbor dirt and parasites. Pieces of bark, clay plant pots, or flat rocks make useful hiding places for the secretive species and become microenvironments where animals can seek out cooler or damper areas if they wish.

Equipping the invertebrate cage

In the wild, invertebrates have some control over the conditions under which they live - they can move about from place to place according to the temperature, light, humidity, and so on. In captivity, they have only a limited opportunity to do this. It is important, therefore, to monitor their environment closely and, if necessary, to use appropriate equipment to maintain it in the correct way.

Heating the cage

Tropical species must be kept at a suitable temperature if they are to thrive in captivity. Unless the room in which they are housed is maintained at a constant 75-80°F, you must provide some form of supplementary heating. The safest and most convenient method is to place small heat mats beneath the cages. These raise the temperature of the cage about 18°F above that of the ambient temperature and can be controlled by a thermostat if necessary. Each model is slightly different, so it is important to follow the manufacturer's instructions.

Alternative forms of heating include light bulbs, which are cheap and easy to install, but have the disadvantage that the temperature will drop when they are turned off at night. Remember that if they are left on all night, the animals will not receive a natural day and night cycle. Soil-warming cables, as used in horticulture, may be suitable, but they tend to be unnecessarily long unless you anticipate keeping several shelves full of invertebrates.

Lighting the cage

Many invertebrates are secretive, forest-floor creatures that shun bright light and many are nocturnal by nature. Keeping these species in a brightly lit cage will stress them and they will not do well. In a room with a window, supplementary lighting should not be necessary at all, although if you want to watch your pets at night you could fit a low-powered, red light bulb. Invertebrates do not see red light and will therefore continue to behave naturally.

Above: Spiders and scorpions must be kept in a secure enclosure. It should be made of a material that is not easily broken and the lid should clip on firmly.

Right: Place a small heat pad under the cage. Choose a model that looks neat and tidy and is safe to use. Heat pads give out a gentle heat, ideal for most tropical and subtropical invertebrates. Electrical consumption is negligible.

Below: Tropical invertebrates such as this exotic mantid, Choeradolis rhombacollis, *will usually require* some supplementary heating. Many of them come from a humid environment and must also be sprayed every day.

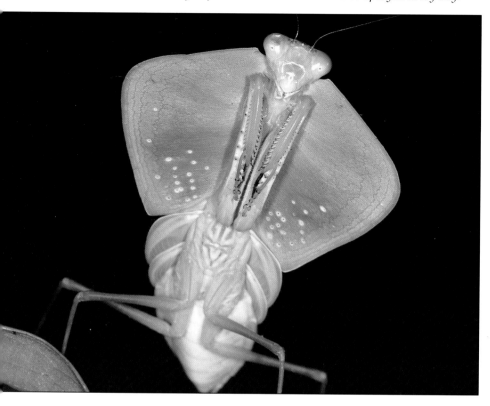

Humidity levels

Many invertebrates have little protection against dehydration and quickly succumb to conditions that are too dry. It is important to establish the correct level of humidity required by each species and to maintain this level by spraying them at regular intervals. The whole cage should be thoroughly misted once or twice each day. Well-ventilated cages obviously dry out much more quickly than those with little ventilation and will need more frequent spraying. However, good air circulation is equally important and you should not allow the atmosphere inside the cage to become stagnant: let your nose be your guide!

Where conditions for a particular species are not well known, it is a good idea to place heating equipment at one end of the cage only, thus creating a temperature gradient, and to spray one area of the cage to create a humidity gradient. This will give the cage inhabitants a wide choice of conditions. If they then spend all their time in one part of the cage, it is safe to assume that the conditions there are to their liking and it may be necessary to redesign the cage or to adjust the environment accordingly.

Using a heat pad

For many exotic pets, the best way to create the right temperature is to place a heat pad controlled by a thermostat under the cage. The thermostat sensor can rest on the heat pad. Put a thermometer inside the cage, just above the substrate. Turn the heater on and turn the thermostat up as far as it will go. When the temperature in the cage is correct, turn the thermostat down until the light goes out. Monitor the temperature in the cage for several hours to ensure that it stays within the correct range. Some trial and error may be necessary before you can establish the right thermostat setting, so it is a good idea to install the cages and equipment before buying any livestock. If you have more than one cage, you should be able to obtain a heat pad to service a number of cages.

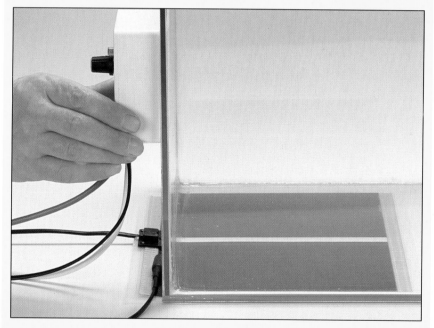

Above: Fix an electronic thermostat to one end of the cage. One lead will go to the mains and another to the heat pad. The third lead has a temperature sensor on the end.

Right: Site the sensor carefully. Here it is installed over the heat pad, the warmest position. If you move it, be sure to recalibrate the thermostat.

Feeding invertebrates

As you consider the various types of invertebrates available, it soon becomes clear that they have a huge range of dietary preferences. Some are more particular than others - indeed, there are species that are hard to keep in captivity because the food they require is difficult or impossible to obtain. Here we consider the general feeding requirements of both herbivorous and predatory species. Detailed feeding advice for individual species accompanies the descriptions on pages 22-49.

Herbivorous species

Species that eat plant material are known as herbivores. These include popular invertebrate pets, such as stick insects, snails, and the larvae, or caterpillars, of butterflies and moths. However, not all these species will eat just any vegetable material. Wild plants have evolved defenses against insects and other predators, usually in the form of chemicals that make their leaves distasteful or poisonous.

Insects, in turn, have developed ways of overcoming these defenses, either by breaking down the chemicals or by storing them in a part of their body where they can do no harm. Usually, each invertebrate is able to cope with just one or two plant poisons and is therefore limited to eating only those plants that contain those chemicals and no others. Plants that contain different chemicals are not palatable. (Incidentally, many insects are also distasteful to *their* predators and they often acquire their chemical defenses from the plants they eat.) The plant or plants that each species of invertebrate will accept is known as its foodplant.

Although the foodplants of many exotic invertebrates are correspondingly exotic themselves, they can often be replaced with more readily available substitutes. For example, most stick insects will accept privet, bramble, or raspberry and many moth larvae also accept privet or ivy. Fortunately, most of these plants are available throughout the year, although it may be necessary to hunt for some of them in sheltered places. Other invertebrates, however, insist on particular foodplants that may be unavailable or available only at certain times of the year. Where the foodplant is seasonal, it may be possible to arrest the development of the animals at a point where they do not require feeding. For example, the pupae of many moths can be kept cool throughout the winter, then warmed up in the spring when their foodplant is in leaf. The emerging adults can then be given the correct foodplant on which to lay their eggs and their caterpillars will not go hungry.

To keep foodplants fresh in the cage, place their stems in a small jar of water. However, if the insects are small, they sometimes drown in the jar. If there is any danger of this happening, plug the jar with absorbent cotton or fill it with a material such as vermiculite that will absorb all the surplus water.

Silkmoth food plants

Species	Preferred food	Emergency food
Japanese moonmoth (*Actias artemis*)	Oak	Cherry
American moonmoth (*Actias luna*)	Birch	Walnut
Indian moonmoth (*Actias selene*)	Rhododendron	Hawthorn, willow laurel
Japanese oak silkmoth (*Antheraea yamamai*)	Oak	
Giant atlas moth (*Attacus atlas*)	Privet	Willow
Bullseye moth (*Autometis io*)	Hawthorn, oak	Willow, privet
Cherry moth (*Callosamia promethea*)	Cherry	Birch
Horned devil (*Citheronia brisotti*)	Privet	
Robin moth (*Hyalophora cecropia*)	Apple	Cherry
Emperor moth (*Saturnia pavonia*)	Birch, bramble	Hawthorn

Left: *Fruit flies,* Drosophila, *are a good food for the smallest invertebrates. Transferring them to the cage will be easier if you first chill the fruit flies in a refrigerator for a few minutes.*

Right: *Silkmoth caterpillars can be quite fussy about their foodplant. Make sure that the species you buy will eat a plant species that grows locally, because they require enormous quantities of it.*

Predatory species

Certain invertebrates are predatory. Because of their small size, their prey is usually limited to small insects and you will have to either buy or breed a suitable food species. On pages 30-31 you will find instructions for keeping and breeding crickets and locusts; although these creatures may be kept solely for their own interest, they are also excellent food animals. Fruit flies, *Drosophila*, are a good food for very small predatory invertebrates, such as newly hatched praying mantids. You can buy ready-made cultures from which a few flies will emerge each day until the culture medium is used up and then order another batch. Mealworms and waxworms are the larval forms of a beetle and a moth, respectively. They are usually available through pet stores or specialist dealers and are a suitable food for larger predatory species, such as spiders. Finally, it may be possible to collect some small invertebrates from the garden or waste ground. Aphids are often available in large numbers on rose bushes and other garden plants; the easiest way of gathering them is to pick the sprigs on which they have congregated. You can use a strong butterfly net or a sweep net to harvest large numbers of small bugs by swishing the net backwards and forwards through long grass and weeds. Always make absolutely sure that no potentially dangerous species, such as predatory wasps or large spiders, are accidentally introduced to the cage, along with the food species.

Hawkmoth food plants

US species ("sphinxes")	Preferred food	Emergency food
Hog sphinx (*Darapsa myron*)	Grapevine, Virginia creeper	Willowherb
Wild cherry sphinx (*Sphinx drupiferarum*)	Cherry, plum, apple	
Large poplar sphinx (*Pachysphinx modesta*)	Willow, poplar	
Poplar sphinx (*Pachysphinx occidentalis*)	Willow, poplar	

European species ("hawkmoths")	Preferred food	Emergency food
Death's head hawkmoth (*Acherontia atropos*)	Privet	
Privet hawkmoth (*Sphinx ligustri*)	Privet	Lilac, ash
Lime hawkmoth (*Mimus tiliae*)	Elm, lime, birch	
Eyed hawkmoth (*Smerinthus ocellata*)	Willow, apple	
Elephant hawkmoth (*Deilephila elpenor*)	Willowherb, bedstraw	
Small elephant hawkmoth (*Deilephila porcellus*)	Willowherb, bedstraw	

Collecting food

If you collect food for your invertebrates, make sure that the area in which you are collecting has not been sprayed with insecticides or herbicides. This applies to plant material and insects. If you are collecting in your own garden, there should be no problem, but collecting on waste ground can be risky. Buying food from a reliable outlet is the safest option.

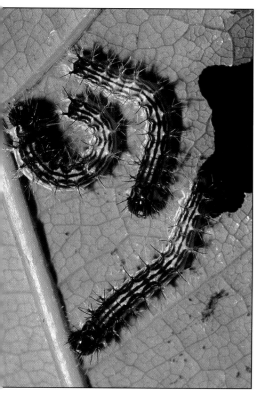

Right: Mantids are voracious predators. This Sphodromantis *species is eating a cricket not much smaller than itself and it will require two or three of these insects each day to thrive.*

21

Stick insects

Stick insects and their relatives are popularly known as "phasmids." Phasmids are found throughout the world, usually in tropical or subtropical countries, and they are masters of disguise. As their name suggests, most species look like sticks - and they are easily thrown away when their foodplant is changed - but others imitate dead or living leaves and some even mimic other insects.

Housing

Stick insects are easy to care for, inexpensive, and long-lived. Most species will breed readily in captivity, so you can keep a small colony going indefinitely. You can house stick insects in any of the insect cages described on pages 16-17, but large species require fairly tall cages, at least twice their own height, so that they can molt properly. They will live at room temperature, but are most active at about 68-73°F. Most of the available species eat common foodplants and you can cut small branches of suitable species and place them in a small jar of water, where they will remain fresh for several days. Plug the top of the jar to avoid the risk of the insects crawling in and drowning. When the leaves of the foodplant begin to wither, collect new pieces and discard the old ones - but not before carefully searching for immobile stick insects! Give the cage a light spray every day to raise the humidity.

Below: Indian stick insects, Carausius morosus, *thrive under a variety of conditions and on a range of foodplants. There are no males in this species.*

Right: Heteropteryx dilatata, *the jungle nymph. This stick insect is easily kept in captivity and one of the largest and longest-lived of all insect species.*

Breeding

Most people start by keeping the common Indian stick insect, *Carausius morosus*. It is easily fed on privet, bramble or ivy and reaches an adult size of about 4in. This species is interesting because only females are present - they grow up, mature and start laying eggs without having any contact with a male. The eggs hatch after about four months and produce another generation of females. This reproductive system is known as "parthenogenesis." Several other stick insect species are also parthenogenetic, but many are not.

If you want to breed non-parthenogenetic stick insects, you must keep males as well as females. Females are usually larger than males, and in some species only the males have wings. Mating takes place shortly after the final molt and the male and female often stay together for several days.

The eggs are like small rounded seeds, varying in size, shape, and color according to the species. If you look at them closely, you may see a small swelling at one end. This is the lid, or "capitulum," through which the baby stick insect will emerge. Females lay several hundred eggs throughout their adult life. These drop to the floor of the cage and are easily lost among the debris. You should attempt to gather some of the eggs in order to keep the colony going and the easiest way to do this is to tip the contents of the cage onto a piece of white paper and sort through it with a small paintbrush. If you find any eggs, place them in a small plastic box with a shallow layer of moist sand on the bottom and keep them at the same temperature as the adults. The box should have a few small holes in the lid for ventilation. The eggs may take an enormous length of time to hatch - over one year in some species. When the eggs begin to hatch, remove the lid and place the plastic box in a new cage with some foodplant. The babies will climb up the cage until they find the food. Stick insect nymphs are not as tough as adults and it is vital that you spray them every day.

Below: A half-grown female jungle nymph. Males are brown and more slender. Breeding this species is not difficult but you will need patience, as the nymphs are slow-growing and the eggs seem to take forever to hatch!

A selection of species

The pink-winged stick insect is rather similar to the Indian stick insects, but the nymphs are bright green. Although this species develops wings in its adult stage, it is a weak flier and captives are easy to control. It eats raspberry leaves and brambles, and the females attach their eggs to the sides of the cage. Of the many other species seen in captivity, Macleay's specter, *Extatosoma tiaratum*, is one of the more spectacular. This Australian species is much larger than the common stick insect and females will grow to 4.7in. long, although males are smaller and much more slender. Only the males have wings. The nymphs have a black body and orange head and are said to mimic certain species of biting ants. As they grow, their color changes to light brown. Adults are remarkable for the frills, flaps, and short spines that cover most of their legs and bodies. This species feeds on brambles and raspberry leaves and is easy to rear.

Once the stick insect bug has bitten, so to speak, there are many other species available to the specialist. Some of these are not quite as straightforward to care for as the Indian stick insect, for instance, but should not present any real difficulties. The jungle nymph, *Heteropteryx dilatata*, comes from Malaysia. This is a truly enormous insect, with females reaching 6.2in. and males only slightly less. It has a much thicker body than many other stick insects and large females can weigh up to 1.76oz., making them among the heaviest of all insects. Both sexes are well armed with prickly spines, but whereas the males are brown with large, dark-colored wings, the females are bright green and have no wings. This species is most easily fed on bramble or oak leaves. Because it requires a humid environment, keep it in an enclosed cage, not one made of mesh. It is a very long-lived species, taking about 18 months to become adult and then living for another year or so. Its egg-laying habits are unusual in that the female buries her large eggs in the ground, so to breed this species successfully, provide a substrate of peat or leaf-litter. Dig the eggs out of the

Left: A bizarre stick insect from Borneo, probably belonging to the genus Dares. *Several unusual stick insects have been introduced in recent years and make highly individual pets. This is an adult and a nymph of two months.*

Right: A leaf insect, Phyllium celebicum, *one of nature's most remarkable examples of camouflage. These creatures make interesting and attractive subjects for a display cage.*

peat every few weeks and place them in fresh peat in a small plastic box. They hatch after 12-18 months and the nymphs are easy to rear.

Stick insects belonging to the genus *Dares* have no widely accepted common name, but are interesting and easy to rear. The three species in culture all grow to about 2in. long and their bodies are covered with long spines. They are dark brown in color and males often have a wide cream, brown, or orange stripe down their backs. Neither sex has wings. These species also require high humidity and are easy to keep in plant propagators or cylindrical "larvae" cages. Their foodplant is bramble or raspberry.

Leaf insects

At first glance, the leaf insects do not look as though they are closely related to stick insects. Indeed, they do not even look as though they are part of the animal kingdom! They are among the most highly modified of all insects and have evolved to look exactly like the leaves of the plants on which they feed, even down to details such as small brown-edged holes where the "leaf" has been nibbled!

All leaf insects belong to the genus *Phyllium* and come from Southeast Asia. Although there are a number of species, they vary only slightly in appearance. As the care and breeding of all species is much the same, accurate identification is not too important. In captivity, leaf insects will eat bramble and, sometimes, oak leaves, although their preferred foodplants are tropical species, such as guava. The most critical time is immediately after the young have hatched: only a proportion of them will accept bramble, etc. and some losses are almost bound to occur. To make certain of success with these insects, it is best to buy nymphs that have already started feeding. Since they live for a long time, starting with half-grown nymphs is quite a viable proposition.

Leaf insects require warm, humid conditions, so spray their cage frequently. It is also a good idea to keep a few stick insects in the same cage because they will nibble at the edges of the foodplant leaves and the leaf insects seem more inclined to feed on leaves that have already been attacked. Alternatively, snip off the tips of the leaves with a pair of scissors. Leaf insects are red when they hatch and then turn brown or green. Sometimes there is a color difference between males and females or the color may depend on the temperature, humidity, or on the health of the insects. Both sexes develop wings after their final molt, but females are normally larger than males, with shorter antennae. Some females will lay eggs without having mated, but at other times the presence of males is essential. Treat the eggs in the same way as those of stick insects and they should hatch in 6 to 12 months. Keeping a colony of leaf insects going for any length of time is quite a challenge, but they are among the most bizarre and interesting insects and well worth the effort.

Praying mantids

About 2,000 species of praying mantids are found throughout the tropical and subtropical parts of the world. They are some of the most wonderfully adapted insects, hiding among leaves, twigs, and flowers and lying in wait for one of their smaller relatives to blunder within range. Then they strike quickly, using their spiky forelegs to grasp their prey and cling on as they devour it piecemeal.

Feeding mantids

All praying mantids are insectivorous and can handle prey almost their own size. In captivity, they will be content with a diet of crickets, locusts, or flies. Young mantid nymphs must be kept separately, as they are cannibalistic. House them in tall plastic beakers with a mesh lid; the lid can simply be a circle of nylon netting, held in place with a rubber band. Each beaker should contain a small twig for the mantid to cling to, and be sprayed every day so that the mantid can drink. To feed the mantid, simply place small insects in the beaker and replenish the supply when they have all been eaten. Some mantids will accept food from forceps and this can be a more satisfactory feeding method, as every mantid is sure to get at least one meal each day. As they grow, the nymphs will need larger cages and can be kept most satisfactorily in the "larvae" type cylindrical cages or in a small square or cylindrical mesh cage. Remember that mesh cages dry out more quickly than enclosed ones, so they will need more frequent spraying.

The molt

The mantid will molt as it grows and becomes adult after about six months and five or six molts. At this point, the wings appear. Males are much more slender than females and may also be smaller overall. In some species the males are rather sticklike and brown, whereas the females are more leaflike and green. Other species can vary in color and may look like dead leaves or even small orchid flowers.

Breeding

Breeding mantids is not a task for the fainthearted! Males are frequently eaten, sometimes before they have had a chance to mate, sometimes during mating and, very often, straight after mating. On odd occasions, the male escapes and can then mate with another female, but his luck usually runs out on the second or third mating. If you only have one male, and want to keep him alive as long as possible, try giving the female a large meal just before introducing the male. His

Above: The orchid mantid comes from Southeast Asia. It mimics flowers in order to attract butterflies and other potential prey. The one pictured here is a young nymph. If placed on a magnolia flower, this species practically disappears before your eyes.

Left: A brown Sphodromantis *species that is easily reared in captivity. Mantids of this genus are among the most commonly available species; some are green whereas others are brown, but it can be difficult putting a name to them all.*

26

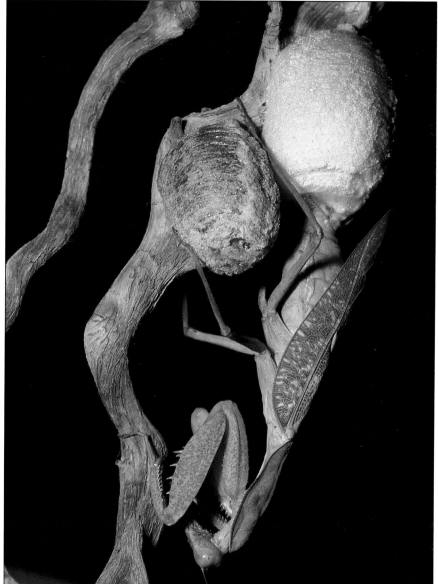

Above: Male mantids are smaller than females and cling to the female's back during mating. Females often eat their mates if they get the chance, so watch them carefully when you first introduce them. If necessary, remove the male and reintroduce him a few days later.

Right: The female lays several egg masses, starting about two weeks after mating. They are soft and sticky at first, but soon harden off. Keep them in tall, ventilated jars, where they remain pinned to the lid until they hatch. This species is Hierodula trimaculata.

chances of survival will also depend on the timing. The female is most likely to want to mate about two weeks after her final molt; if the male is introduced before this, she will probably assume that he is just one more meal. Similarly, if the male tries to escape from the cage as soon as he senses the female, the chances of a productive mating are not good - the male can usually sense whether or not the female is receptive and will only approach her if she is.

Mantids lay their eggs as oothecae, or egg-cases. Each female will lay about six oothecae, even though she may have mated only once. In the more common species, each ootheca is about the size of a walnut and after it has dried it has the consistency of hard foam. Each one contains up to 300 eggs, depending on the species and the size of the female, and if it is kept at about 73-77°F will usually hatch after about two months. The baby mantids are tiny and at first they can only feed on the very smallest types of livefoods, such as fruit flies (Drosophila), hatchling crickets, aphids, etc. Most breeders keep the young mantids together for a few days; in this way, they will feed on one another, with the weaker individuals providing meals for the stronger ones. Once the nymphs are reduced to manageable numbers, place them in separate beakers as already described, and the cycle will start once more.

Right: All the eggs in the ootheca hatch at the same time. The tiny nymphs crawl out of the egg-case and lower themselves to the ground on threads. They molt their skins within minutes of hatching and immediately begin to look for food. At this stage they are very cannibalistic and their numbers will be greatly reduced unless they are well fed. This can be an advantage, as it saves you keeping several hundred nymphs.

Cockroaches

Cockroaches belong to the family Blattidae and are closely related to the mantids. Although the more common species, notably the American cockroach, *Periplaneta americana*, are less than lovable, several of the tropical species are relatively slow-moving and can make extremely interesting and entertaining pets. All cockroaches are nocturnal and become active during the evening. This is the best time to observe and enjoy them.

Housing

The housing requirements of cockroaches are fairly basic. A small plastic cage is adequate, but will require some form of heating unless it is kept in a permanently warm room. A small undercage heat pad, producing a temperature in the range 68-77°F, is the best arrangement. A naturalistic set-up using soil and dead leaves will suit cockroaches, but it is easier to keep them clean on a layer of newspaper or kitchen paper, sprinkled with a thin layer of sawdust if required. Cockroaches prefer confined spaces, so place a stack of folded cardboard or fiber egg-boxes in their cage; during the day they will wedge themselves into the nooks and crannies between the layers and by night they will clamber over the vertical and horizontal surfaces.

Feeding

Cockroaches eat almost anything - this has been the key to their success - but in the interests of hygiene and convenience, feed them on pieces of fresh fruit, especially apple and banana, supplemented with pelleted rabbit food. Change the fruit every day or two or it will become moldy. Supply water in a small container stuffed with damp absorbent cotton or spray the cockroaches every day, but do not allow the cage to become too damp, as this encourages mites and other parasites.

Species of interest

The Madagascan hissing cockroach, *Gromphadorhina madagascariensis*, is probably the most frequently kept species. As its name suggests, it is capable of producing a hissing sound designed to startle possible predators. The sound is produced by expelling air through the spiracles - a series of small pores along the sides of all insects through which they "breathe." In time, frequently handled specimens will refuse to hiss. Hissing cockroaches have no wings and are shiny black or dark reddish-brown. They are among the largest species of cockroaches, eventually growing to 2.75-3.2in. long.

Above: The nymphs of Cuban cockroaches, Byrsotria fumigata, *are circular, but become more elongated as they grow. Males have wings and grow to about 1.5in. long, whereas females have no wings but are slightly larger.*

Above: The West Indian cockroach, Blaberus craniifer, *is one of several species sometimes called "leaf" cockroaches. Only the adults have wings. Tropical cockroaches are quite slow moving and do not become household pests should they escape.*

Left: A Madagascan hissing cockroach, Gromphadorhina *species. This cockroach is a favorite with children, because it hisses loudly when touched. It is a large species, growing to more than 2in. long and the males have a pair of prominent "horns" just behind their heads. Like all the species illustrated here, it gives birth to living young. If you suspect a female is pregnant, make sure there are no gaps through which the young might escape - they are much smaller than the adults!*

Males are broader than females and have two lumps, or "horns," on their pronotum - the shield immediately behind their head.

Another large species, the Cuban cockroach, *Byrsotria fumigata*, differs in having wings, even though it rarely flies. This species is brown, with darker markings. There are several other similar species in tropical regions and their care is identical to that described above.

Breeding

Breeding cockroaches is not difficult - indeed, they tend to breed whether you encourage them or not! All the species mentioned are livebearing and their reproduction is quite interesting. Mating takes place with the male and female joined "end to end." At this time, the eggs are already beginning to develop inside the female's body. A few weeks later they are partially expelled, and look rather like a small yellow corn cob protruding from the back of the female's abdomen. Then they are withdrawn again, and in the process they are turned and fertilized by the stored spermatazoa. Development then resumes inside the female's body and a brood of up to 20 nymphs is born some weeks later. At first, they are white and soft-skinned, but they soon harden and turn brown. They can be left with the adults or moved to a separate cage for rearing. The young nymphs of *Byrsotria* and related species are especially striking - they look very much like tiny prehistoric trilobytes.

Crickets and locusts

Although crickets and locusts are hardly "pets," they are worth keeping on two counts. Firstly, they are easy to breed, even with very little space, time, or money. This makes them ideal insects to keep in schools, for example, where their life cycle can be studied easily and within a relatively short space of time. Secondly, crickets and locusts are ideal food insects for other exotic pets, such as large spiders, praying mantids, amphibians, and reptiles.

Below: The common house cricket, Acheta domestica, *is found throughout the world. It makes a good food species for larger insects, spiders, amphibians, and reptiles.*

Housing

Crickets and locusts have rather similar requirements, but crickets are slightly less troublesome. The house cricket, *Acheta domestica*, is the species most often bred, but another species, the field cricket, *Gryllus bimaculatus*, is larger and more attractive. It also has the advantage of not setting up its home in your home should it escape from its enclosure!

Below: The field cricket, Gryllus bimaculatus, *is not as prolific as the house cricket, but grows larger. It is the best species to keep, unless you require large numbers for feeding to other pets.*

You can house crickets in a plastic aquarium or a large plastic food container with ventilation panels. As long as the sides are kept clean and smooth the crickets will not be able to climb them but, of course, they may jump out unless you fit a lid. Crickets are not too fussy about temperature but will be most active - and grow most rapidly - if they are kept reasonably warm at, say, 68-77°F. However, this is not critical and there is no need to install expensive heating equipment.

Male crickets are territorial, so increase the surface living space by making a stack of fiber egg-boxes, cardboard tubes, or crumpled brown paper. You could cover the floor of the cage with a layer of sawdust or fine sand but this is not strictly necessary. If the insects are on display, then pieces of bark and a layer of dead leaves fulfill the territorial requirements and make a more attractive set-up.

Feeding

Crickets will eat flaked fish food, crumbled biscuits, wholemeal bread, and the meal sold for chicks and hens. Slices of fruit and vegetable are also accepted, but change them daily so that they do not become moldy. Supply drinking water by stuffing a shallow bowl with damp absorbent cotton or a piece of foam rubber.

Breeding

Wings do not develop until the crickets' final molt. By this time it will be easy to distinguish between the males and the females, as the latter have long, swordlike ovipositors sticking out of the end of their abdomens. In addition, only the males sing. They do this by rubbing the edges of their wings together, which produces a chirping or buzzing sound. Crickets are most active at night. Although their song is not unpleasant it can be somewhat monotonous - once they start singing you may decide to move them to a part of the home that is well away from the bedrooms!

After they have mated, the females will need a suitable place to lay their eggs, such as a shallow dish containing either moistened peat, sand, or vermiculite. They use their long ovipositors to place the eggs well below the surface and, if several females are laying in the same cage, you should provide a new egg-laying container every day to prevent each one from becoming overcrowded.

When you have removed the egg-laying tray from the cage, cover it to prevent the substrate from drying out. Put it in a warm place - 68-77°F is ideal - and the eggs will hatch in two to four weeks. The tiny crickets will find their way to the surface of the dish and can be transferred to a fresh cage and given some food and water. They grow quickly and may reach maturity in eight to ten weeks if they are well fed and kept reasonably warm. Crickets are amazingly prolific - unless they are needed as live food for other pets, it is a good idea to dispose of a proportion of the nymphs each generation.

Locusts

Two species of locusts are frequently bred in schools and laboratories, namely the migratory locust, *Locusta migratoria*, and the desert locust, *Schistocerca gregaria*. The care and breeding of both species is similar and both make excellent live food for larger lizards, spiders, and so on.

Locusts require taller cages than crickets and a diet of fresh greenstuff, grass being the best. They are rather more cold-sensitive than crickets and many commercial locust cages have a fitting for a small light bulb to maintain a suitable temperature of about 77°F. Females need a deep substrate for egg-laying - a glass jar filled with damp sand is ideal - and you should place several of these jars in the cage once the locusts have reached maturity. The eggs are laid towards the bottom of the jar and are connected to the surface with a column of foam, allowing the hatchling locust hoppers to eat their way to the surface when they hatch. Change the jars every day or two and cover any jar containing eggs with a ventilated lid before storing it in a warm place. The eggs hatch after two to four weeks and then you can transfer the hoppers to a clean cage. They require the same care as the adults.

Above: The migratory locust, Locusta migratoria, *is the species most commonly kept in schools and laboratories. The larger lizard species are especially fond of these insects.*

Below: The desert locust, Schistocerca gregaria, *is a colorful species of locust, especially as a nymph. It breeds readily, but is not as common in captivity as the migratory locust.*

31

Silkmoths

Many people are surprised to learn how easy it is to keep moths in captivity. Although a number of moths can be kept successfully, the most interesting species are the silkmoths and the hawkmoths, or sphinxes. Silkmoths include all those species that make a silky cocoon, and they are placed together in the family Saturniidae. The family includes the moonmoths, atlas moths, and bullseye moths, among others. Most species are large, brightly colored and have prominent feathery antennae. The adults of most species have no functional mouthparts and do not feed. They live for only a few weeks - or even a few days - as adults, and put their main effort into rearing the caterpillars.

Caterpillars can sometimes be collected from the wild (provided they are not protected), but wild caterpillars are often parasitized. Since many dealers in insects can supply eggs, caterpillars and pupae at certain times of the year, this is a much safer way of acquiring stock.

Most silkmoth caterpillars, even exotic species, feed on readily available foodplants such as cherry, oak, and willow. However, these foodplants are seasonal, so take care to synchronize the life cycle of the moths with the availability of the foodplants, otherwise the adults may lay their eggs at a time of year when there is nothing for the young caterpillars to eat when they hatch out.

Above and left: Silkmoths and related species, such as these moonmoths, Actia luna, are at their best when they first emerge from their pupae; being clumsy fliers, they quickly damage themselves by fluttering about in their cage. The scales that gives the wings their color are soon lost and, in particular, the long "tails" of their hind wings become ragged after just a few hours, as seen here.

Left: Silkmoth caterpillars weave an intricate, silky cocoon. Callosamia promethea even incorporates dead leaves. Overwinter the chrysalids of this species or they will emerge when there is no food for the next generation.

Above: Cricula trifenestrata is one of several species with small transparent "windows" in their wings. These are areas where there are no scales to give them color. All the windowed silkmoths are tropical, but easy to rear and breed.

Breeding

Assuming that you have obtained eggs from a breeder or dealer in the spring, place them next to some leaves of the appropriate foodplant. In fact, the eggs may have been supplied on leaves. The foodplant may consist of a few stems of the appropriate species standing in a small jar of water or it may be more convenient to place a growing plant, in its pot, in the cage with the eggs.

Once the caterpillars hatch, they will eat their own eggshells and then begin to crawl around looking for their foodplant. As soon as they find something to their liking, they will start to feed and holes will begin to appear at the edges of the leaves. Once the caterpillars begin to grow, they will molt their skins every few days and their appetites will increase dramatically. The foodplant will disappear before your eyes! Eventually, when the caterpillars have molted six or seven times, they will begin to look for a suitable place to pupate.

As a rule, silkmoth caterpillars pupate among the leaves of the foodplant, making a characteristic pupa surrounded in a cocoon of silk. Remove the pupae from the cage and place them in a plastic box. Species such as the Indian moonmoth can be fed on rhododendron all the year round, and if their pupae are kept warm they will hatch after three or four weeks. If they pupate early enough in the year, keep the pupae warm and it may be possible to produce two generations in a single season. However, other species require food that is not always available, such as banana or guava leaves. In this case, keep the pupae in a cool place until the following spring, when their foodplant will again be available. Then you can warm them up and allow them to emerge. This should take place inside a large cage with mesh sides. Lay the pupae on the bottom of the cage and spray them every other day. When the adults emerge, they will climb up the sides of the cage and hang down, allowing their wings enough room to expand and dry without becoming crumpled.

Hawkmoths

The family of hawkmoths is found throughout the world and is known as the Sphingidae. The adults are strong fliers and many of them are active during the day, when they look like bees or tiny birds as they hover in front of flowers sipping the nectar. They typically have narrow, pointed wings and a streamlined body. Some are brightly colored, but others have more subtle markings to help them to blend with the vegetation on which they rest. The caterpillars of many species are beautifully marked and take up rather strange postures - hence the Latin name of the family and the American common name of "sphinx moths." Hawkmoths present rather more of a challenge to their keeper than silkmoths, but are not difficult to rear if you are prepared to go to a little trouble. The basic techniques are the same for both groups of species.

Breeding
Although hawkmoth caterpillars can sometimes be found in large numbers, most people will find it easier to buy some eggs or larvae from an insect dealer. These require the same care as the eggs and larvae of silkmoths, but be sure to obtain the correct foodplant for the species you have bought.

When the larvae are fully grown their behavior will change. They stop feeding, become darker and shrink slightly. These are signs that they are ready to pupate. Some species pupate on the surface, whereas others burrow. In order to allow for either type of behavior, fill a plastic food container or a small plastic aquarium with a 6in. layer of sieved soil with added fiber (coconut fiber, or coir, is ideal). Add a layer of dead leaves to the top of the compost. Put the larvae in the container and after two or three weeks they should have pupated, either well below the surface or in the dead leaves. Be careful not to damage them when rummaging through the soil. Now place them in a small plastic tub lined with tissue or cotton and keep them in a cool environment, ideally at about 39-46°F. Leave them until the following spring.

When they are due to emerge, move the box containing the pupae into a tall mesh cage so that the moths can crawl up the sides and expand their wings as soon as they emerge. Once their wings have dried, you can gently handle the moths by placing a finger just under the head and encouraging them to crawl onto it. Day-flying species should only be handled during the night and vice versa, otherwise they will take off and may damage themselves by crashing into walls, windows, and other objects.

Although some species are rather difficult to breed, many will pair and lay eggs in a small breeding cage, as described for the silkmoths. Lime, poplar, and

Above: The bright body colors of the privet sphinx, Sphinx ligustri, *are exposed only if the camouflage of their upper wings fails to fool a predator.*

Left: The caterpillar of the death's-head hawkmoth, Acherontia atropos. *Because of the posture assumed by the larvae, they may be called "sphinxes."*

Above: A selection of sphinx pupae, or chrysalids. Although they vary in size, all the species in this family form a characteristic brown, pointed pupa.

Above: The elephant hawkmoth, Deilephila elepenor, *is small but beautifully marked. It is named for its caterpillars, which are gray and look like elephants' trunks. Their foodplant is willowherb.*

Other suitable moths

The familiar "woolly bear" caterpillars are the larvae of the tiger moth, with several species in Europe and North America. Ermine moths are closely related to tiger moths and you can rear both wherever their caterpillars are found. Their foodplants vary slightly, but they are not too fussy. When the caterpillar pupates, it incorporates its shed hairs into the pupa case. Over-winter the pupae in a cool place and release the newly emerged moths the following spring.

eyed hawkmoths have no mouthparts and do not feed. The males and females of these species can simply be placed together as soon as they have emerged and pairing will take place shortly afterwards. Take care not to disturb the moths while they are paired. When they have separated, place the female in a small, dark box such as a cardboard shoebox or a plastic box lined with nylon mesh. Only place one female in each laying box. The female will lay her eggs over the next few days and they can be transferred to larval rearing cages containing the appropriate foodplant.

Species other than those mentioned above should be fed before they pair or lay eggs. Place flowers containing plenty of nectar in the breeding cage with them (honeysuckle is popular, but there are several other good species).

If all this sounds a little complicated, there is another way of enjoying hawkmoths. This is to buy a batch of larvae from a breeder or dealer at the beginning of the year, rear them until they pupate, overwinter them and then release them in the spring. If you grow the right foodplants for them in your garden, the moths may remain long enough to breed and, hopefully, establish a natural population. However, it is very important not to release species that do not naturally occur in your area, nor to release specimens reared from "foreign" stock that may not be as well adapted as members of the local population. Secondly, it is vital to make sure that the moths emerge at the right time of the year, i.e. when the correct foodplant is available, otherwise they will have nowhere to lay their eggs.

Butterflies

As a rule, butterflies are more trouble to keep than moths because they are strong fliers and require large cages. Most serious breeders devote greenhouses or large outdoor mesh "aviaries" to housing them. However, you can raise many local species, either by collecting the caterpillars or by buying them from breeders, including butterfly farms. If you rear locally occurring species, you can eventually release them, thus helping to boost local populations and, possibly, encouraging small colonies in your garden or in local parks or woodlands. Never release species that are not found locally.

Field guides and reference books will help you identify the foodplants of the various species and it is sometimes possible to find newly laid eggs, once you know which plants to look on and what the eggs look like. You can then pick the plants complete with eggs - but only if the plants are common species growing outside national parks and other protected areas. Starting with eggs avoids the risk of acquiring parasitized larvae and allows you to observe the complete process of metamorphosis from egg to adult. Some butterflies overwinter as pupae and will not emerge until the following spring.

Above: The morpho butterflies are among the largest and most spectacular tropical species. This species, Morpho peleides, comes from Costa Rica and is best left to the more experienced insect-breeders as it needs a large flight area.

Left: The bizarre caterpillar of this tropical swallowtail, Atrophaneura, feeds on Aristolochia leaves. The caterpillars of other tropical butterflies eat passion flower or banana leaves, for example. Consult your supplier about exactly which plants to find or grow.

Right: The giant swallowtail, Papilio cresphontes, is a native American species. If you find caterpillars of species such as this, you may like to raise them in your home and release them when they have emerged as adults, thus helping local populations. Do not take caterpillars of rare or protected species.

Spiders

Keeping large spiders has become an increasingly popular part of the interest in exotic pets. The spiders most frequently seen in the pet trade are popularly known as "tarantulas" or "bird-eating spiders" and they are characterized by a large abdomen, stout legs, and large fangs. They are known scientifically as theraphosid spiders (they belong to the family Theraphosidae) and there are approximately 800 known species.

Most tarantulas in the pet trade are collected from the wild, but some species, including the popular Mexican red-kneed tarantula, are now protected in their country of origin. A number of species are regularly bred in captivity, so there should be a ready supply of young spiderlings at reasonable prices and this is the best way to build up a collection.

Because tarantulas do not fit into the generally accepted definition of "pets," there are a few points to bear in mind before starting out. Firstly, although some species are naturally tame and can be handled quite freely by experts, many of them are aggressive and can give a painful bite. Secondly, many species are armed with hairs on their abdomens. The spiders can flick these off if they are upset, causing irritation and allergic reactions. It is therefore essential that cages are totally secure so that there is no risk of any spiders escaping and terrorizing the neighborhood. Finally, remember that children should never be allowed to touch or handle any large spider.

Handling spiders

Even tame spiders should be handled as little as possible to avoid the risk of damaging the spider, as much as to avoid bites. Fortunately, most large spiders are fairly slow-moving except when they are upset, and then they can show a surprising turn of speed over short distances. When cleaning out the spider enclosure, the best arrangement is to have a spare cage ready so that you can carefully encourage the spider to walk from one to

the other. Alternatively, persuade it to enter a small tub or box and hold it there until the old cage has been cleaned. Very aggressive spiders can be caught by placing a plastic beaker over them, making sure that their legs are not damaged. Then slide a piece of stiff card or plastic under the upturned container, thus trapping the spider. When the time comes to replace the spider, put the container inside the cage on its side and slowly remove the piece of card or plastic. Finally, replace the lid of the cage. The container can be retrieved later on, once the spider has left it.

Below: The red-rumped tarantula, Brachypelma vagans, is a colorful and attractive species that is easily reared in captivity. It has a fairly calm temperament and, as a result, is among the species especially recommended for beginners to spider-keeping. Even so, please do not touch!

Right: The red-kneed tarantula, Euathlus smithi, is one of the most beautiful spiders, but wild populations are protected. However, captive-bred spiderlings are sometimes available and this is the best way of building up a collection.

The molt

Baby spiders molt their skins every few weeks, larger ones rather less frequently. Just before molting, the spider becomes much less active and may lose much of the hair on its abdomen. Some species lie upside down immediately before molting and may appear to be dead at first glance. Resist the temptation to prod or pick them up. The old skin should come away in one piece; problems with molting can usually be put down to incorrect conditions, especially a dry environment. It is a good idea to spray the cage lightly every day when a spider looks as though it is approaching a molt.

When spiders are about to molt, they will stop feeding altogether. Do not offer them food at this time, because crickets, in particular, may attack and damage - or even kill - a spider that is in the process of molting. After molting, the spider's colors will be especially bright and any hairs that were lost will be replaced. A healthy spider sheds its skin in one piece, complete with fangs. If you want to collect the old skins, place them carefully in clear plastic boxes where they will be safe from damage. Label the boxes containing the old skins with the name of the species from which they came and the date they were shed.

Housing spiders

Because they are cannibalistic, you must keep spiders singly, except for breeding purposes. This rule applies equally to baby spiders and to adults, although the latter will obviously have to be introduced to each other for breeding purposes.

Tarantulas are best kept in unbreakable containers with lids that can be securely screwed or clipped on. House adult specimens in a plastic vivarium of the type sold for small pets or in a transparent plastic food container. If you use a food container, drill a series of small ventilation holes in the sides or lid or cut out a circular hole with a drill and cover it with a small piece of wire mesh. Young tarantulas can also be housed in food containers, such as plastic beakers with snap- or screw-on lids or in clear plastic specimen tubes. All these containers will need ventilation holes. The larvae cages recommended for caterpillars, stick insects, etc., are not secure enough for housing spiders.

Collectors with large numbers of spiders sometimes favor a purpose-built glass vivarium, divided into a number of compartments, or cells, but there is no real advantage to this arrangement if you only keep a handful of specimens.

Furnishing the vivarium

All spiders are secretive and need somewhere to hide. A small piece of curved cork bark placed on the substrate is the easiest way to create a hiding place. The spider will spin a tunnel-shaped web beneath the bark and spend most of its time at the entrance of the tunnel waiting for food. A few tarantulas are tree-dwellers and they appreciate a tall cage containing an upright tube of cork bark. Make a hole about half way up the bark, big enough for the spider to crawl in and out of.

Humidity level

All spiders, including desert species, need a fairly humid environment. An absorbent material on the floor of the cage will achieve the desired effect. Paper kitchen towels work very well but do not look very natural. A layer of moist vermiculite is slightly better, but the most natural substrate is probably bark chippings, either on its own or over a layer of moist peat moss. This will hold water without becoming waterlogged. Moisten all these substrates when you set up the vivarium and then spray them occasionally to ensure that they do not dry out. Certain types of plastic vivarium

Right: The Indian ornamental spider, Poecilotheria regalis, *is attractively marked, but has a nervous disposition and requires careful treatment. Disturb it as little as possible and, in particular, never pick up a tarantula with your bare hands: apart from anything else, it may be fatally injured if you drop it.*

tend to dry out rather quickly, so it is a good idea to trap a layer of clear polyethylene between part of the top of the cage and the lid. This will help to retain some degree of moisture.

The aim is to create an atmosphere that is humid without being dripping wet. If the humidity is too high, the substrate will become moldy and there is a risk that the spiders will become infected with fungus. If it is too low, they will have trouble in molting their skins. As a rule, there should not be more than a trace of condensation on the lid of the vivarium, so if the sides are constantly wet, reduce the humidity by increasing ventilation and spraying less. Baby spiders will sometimes drown in drops of condensation if the humidity is not properly controlled.

Desert spiders require less humid conditions, so you can dispense with the polyethylene in their enclosures. Keep them on coarse sand or fine aquarium gravel and spray it occasionally. However, this substrate is not suitable for very small spiders, as they may become trapped between the particles.

Heating and lighting

Most tarantulas come from tropical or subtropical regions and require a temperature of 72-83°F. In a normal room, there should be no need to provide additional lighting. Spiders shun brightly lit conditions and will tend to hide away even more than usual.

Above: The pink-toed tarantula, Avicularia avicularia, *is a tropical species that normally lives in holes in trees. It makes a tough and attractive pet and is recommended as a first spider. This climbing species looks most attractive when housed in a tall enclosure with pieces of bark stuck to the back. Provide a hollow upright log in which the spider can make its home. Other species of* Avicularia *are also occasionally available.*

Left: The Chilean rose-haired tarantula, Grammostola gala, *is another good choice for beginners. Other species from Chile are also available from time to time and they all seem to thrive in captivity. However,* G. gala *and its close relative,* G. spatulatus, *are the most popular, as they have especially calm temperaments.*

Below: The goliath spider, Theraphosa leblondi, *is one of the largest spiders in the world. It is very aggressive and does not always fare well in captivity. This species is best left to experts. The best way of avoiding* unsuitable species is to buy from dealers or breeders who specialize in tarantulas. They will be able to advise you on choosing appropriate species and can provide accurate information on all aspects of caring for your spider.

Feeding

All spiders feed on insects. Some of the larger species also eat small vertebrates, such as frogs, lizards, and even small mammals. Despite one of their popular names, very few are capable of catching and eating birds. Captive spiders are almost always fed on insects, such as crickets and locusts.

Newly hatched spiderlings provide a good introduction to spider-keeping. They eat very small insects such as newly hatched crickets or wingless fruit flies, both of which should be available from the dealer who supplies the spiderlings. As the spiders grow, increase the size of their food correspondingly. Cricket and locust nymphs are convenient because they are readily available and come in a continuous range of sizes. Adult spiders will also accept other insects, such as mealworms and waxworms. Remember that large spiders also eat small spiders! Carefully regulate the size of prey items. Spiders can tackle prey that is about one quarter their own size, but if you introduce food that is too large, the spider can become stressed.

Some species have larger appetites than others and you can only assess the amount of food they need by trial and error. Offer spiderlings one or two items of food every other day, but if they leave food from their last meal, reduce the frequency of feeding accordingly. On the other hand, if they seem constantly hungry, increase feeding, either by offering larger meals or by feeding them every day. As they grow, spiders' appetites tend to diminish, so that half-grown spiders require feeding only once or twice each week and adults about once every one or two weeks.

Water

If its cage is maintained at the correct humidity, the spider will rarely need to drink. In addition, its food will contain extra moisture. However, some collectors like to provide additional water in the cage as a safeguard. You can put a small bowl or dish of water in the enclosure, but to avoid the risk of drowning, especially in the case of small spiders, it is safer to fill the dish with wet absorbent cotton or a piece of foam rubber cut to shape.

Breeding

Breeding spiders is a specialized process and best left to experts. Female spiders frequently eat their mates, often before mating has taken place, and it is usually necessary to have a few "reserves" to replace any that end up this way. Another problem is that of telling the sexes apart - spiders can only be sexed reliably once they have reached the adult stage. As a rule, females are significantly larger than males, especially in their abdomens. Females also live longer - sometimes several years as opposed to just a few months.

Scorpions

Contrary to popular belief, not all scorpions are deadly poisonous but most can give a painful sting. The precautions outlined for keeping spiders apply equally to scorpions and there is no excuse whatsoever for allowing them to escape or for handling them casually. A number of species are dangerously poisonous - these are rarely offered for sale and amateurs should never consider keeping them. As there is no way of knowing which are the most dangerous kinds just by looking at them, you must rely on your supplier to identify them correctly. If you are not confident that he or she has the necessary expertise to do this, buy your scorpions elsewhere.

If you have to pick up a scorpion, there is only one safe way to do it. Grasp it firmly just in front of the sting with a pair of long forceps. To avoid damage to the scorpion, it is a good idea to fix small foam pads to the tips of the forceps.

Housing

Scorpions can be kept in a plastic vivarium or a plastic food container. Secure lids are essential. Several species of forest scorpion are available and they require a substrate similar to that recommended for spiders, namely moist vermiculite, peat, or bark chippings. Desert species require drier conditions and should be kept on sand or fine gravel. All scorpions are nocturnal and need a dark place to hide during the day - a suitably sized piece of cork bark laid flat on the substrate is the best means of providing this for all types of scorpion.

Place a heat pad controlled by a thermostat under the cage. The ideal temperature for most species is 73-83°F, but they are fairly tolerant of cooler conditions for short periods of time. Forest species require fairly humid conditions, so spray their cage lightly every other day. Desert species obtain most of their water requirements through their food, but can be sprayed occasionally, provided that their cage is well ventilated.

Feeding

Scorpions eat small insects, such as mealworms, crickets, and locusts. Offer them food two or three times each week; if food remains uneaten from one meal to the next, reduce the amount. Many species are cannibalistic, so house all scorpions separately.

Breeding

Although breeding is a specialized technique, you may occasionally buy a scorpion that is pregnant and then you can observe at first hand the process of caring for the young. All species are livebearers and females give birth to a brood of up to 50 young. At first, the young are white, with soft external skeletons. The mother encourages them to climb onto her back, where she can protect them most easily, and the first sign that a captive scorpion was pregnant is often the appearance of a mass of tiny white babies clinging to their mother's back. Females of some species, such as the emperor scorpion, even provide food for their offspring by killing prey and allowing them to feed from it. However, other species are more inclined to eat their young once they have dispersed after their first molt, so remove the offspring to avoid any such accidents.

Baby scorpions can be reared in captivity, but this is a very time-consuming business. House them individually in small containers, such as plastic freezer boxes, and feed them on the smallest grade of crickets or on fruit flies. They may molt their skins fives times or more before reaching the adult stage and the whole process can take several years in the case of large species.

Above: The imperial scorpion, Pandinus imperator, *is an impressive tropical species that makes a good pet and is the species most often offered for sale. Although basically black, in some lights it looks dark green. It is not aggressive but should never be handled.*

Right: Scorpions can damage your health! This small scorpion from Chile is probably not deadly, but why take a risk when there are better documented species available? Avoid any species that cannot be positively identified and always buy from reputable dealers.

Millipedes and centipedes

Millipedes and centipedes are often sold in pet shops and by dealers in exotic animals. Many of them are difficult to identify, although they may be sold under popular names - often invented by the dealer in order to make them sound more attractive! Be warned, however, that centipedes have painful, sometimes poisonous, bites and only experts should keep them. Millipedes, on the other hand, make good pets and are quite easy to keep. "Giant" millipedes come from warm parts of the world and require some supplementary heating unless housed in a room maintained at a minimum temperature of 68-77°F.

Housing millipedes is straightforward. They only need a fairly small container, such as a small plastic aquarium, fitted with a well-ventilated lid. Cover the base with bark chippings or dead leaves and add one or two larger pieces of bark to create hiding places. Spray the cage lightly every one or two days, but take care that it does not become too damp.

Millipedes are scavengers that eat a wide range of organic material, including decomposing leaves, etc. Small pieces of fruit are probably the most convenient form of food, but remove these after one or two days and replace them with something fresh, otherwise they will become moldy and begin to smell. Supply the millipedes with a variety of food to keep them healthy.

Below: An unidentified millipede from Madagascar. Tropical millipedes come from forested regions and prefer a moist substrate. They eat most plant material. Finding the right conditions for them often involves some guesswork.

Above: Large, vicious centipedes of one sort or another are found in almost every warm part of the world. This is one of the Scolopendra *species from North America. It grows to nearly 6in. long and can deliver a painful bite, but does not have a powerful venom like some of the tropical species. Keep it in a box with a well-fitting lid, some sand or soil and something to hide under. Centipedes are cannibalistic, so house them separately, even if they are of the same species. Move them about as described for spiders (see page 38).*

Centipedes

If you are determined to keep a gruesome species, then centipedes can be housed in similar containers to those recommended for scorpions, but make absolutely sure that the lid fits properly and the cage is secure. **Centipedes are fast-moving and difficult to recapture if they escape.** Unlike millipedes, they are predatory and require a diet of small insects, such as crickets.

Hermit crabs and giant snails

Hermit crabs

Hermit crabs are often available from pet stores or specialist invertebrate dealers. Unfortunately, it is rarely possible to tell which species they belong to, although all require similar care.

Although many hermit crabs are marine, a number of them live along the shoreline, dipping into the ocean every so often or obtaining their moisture from damp sand and rotting vegetation. These species make quite good captives, although they rarely live for very long and have not been known to reproduce in captivity.

A small plastic aquarium makes an ideal container. Cover the floor with clean damp sand, coral gravel, small pebbles, or live sphagnum moss. Thoroughly spray the sides of the cage, as well as the substrate, every day. As a general guide, the available species are invariably tropical, so keep their cage in a warm room or heat it by means of a small heat pad. The ideal temperature is about 77°F. Hermit crabs are scavengers and will eat pieces of fruit, as well as a variety of fish foods, especially blocks of freeze-dried *Tubifex* or shrimp. You can keep a number of hermit crabs in the same enclosure, but it is important to include a few empty shells of varying sizes. These will provide the crabs with alternative "homes" to move into as they grow and this in turn will prevent them from resorting to forcibly evicting one another.

Giant snails

Giant land snails are not, of course, related to hermit crabs. Whereas hermit crabs take over empty shells for their "homes," the land snails produce their own shells. The most interesting species to keep in captivity are the large tropical varieties from Africa and Asia. Their shells can grow as long as 4in. and they are easy to keep and breed in captivity, although keeping a cage containing giant snails clean can be difficult, because the snails produce large amounts of waste, and uneaten food quickly decomposes. By the time they are fully grown, three or four snails will need a cage measuring about 24x12x12in. A large glass or plastic aquarium containing a 2in. layer of fairly coarse pebbles on the bottom and a well-fitting but well-ventilated lid makes a good cage.

Feeding

Giant snails will eat just about any vegetable material, including lettuce and cabbage, but they do best on a variety of foodstuffs, including root vegetables, fruit, and leaves. They also eat garden weeds, such as dandelion and groundsel. Remember to place a block of chalk or cuttlefish bone in the cage so that the snails can obtain the calcium they need to make their shells. Flaked or freeze-dried fish food containing plenty of protein is also a good food supplement. A shallow bowl of bran in one corner of the aquarium will suffice as an emergency food supply. Do not put fresh food directly onto the pebbles, but place it on a shallow plastic tray or the plastic lid of a food tub. In this way, most of the mess will be confined to one small area. Remove the tray every day, wash it carefully and put it back into the cage with a fresh selection of food. Once every week or so, take the snails out of their enclosure and rinse them in tepid water. Take this opportunity to give the pebbles a thorough wash as well.

Breeding

Once the snails are full grown they should start to lay eggs. Since snails are hermaphrodite, any two individuals will breed - each snail is both a male and a female and, although it cannot mate with itself, it can produce both sperm and eggs. The eggs are about the size of a pea (larger in some species) and are easy to see when the snails are cleaned out. Collect the eggs and place them in a small plastic box with a layer of peat, sphagnum moss, or damp paper handkerchiefs on the bottom. The time they take to hatch varies enormously, and depends on the species and the temperature, but is usually about 30 days. Keep the young snails in small plastic boxes at first - they will eat their own eggshells before going off in search of food. This should consist of flaked fish food or a finely chopped mixture of the same food as you offer the adults. Young snails require extra calcium to enable their shells to form properly, so sprinkle powdered cuttlefish bone over each meal.

Above: *Land hermit crabs come in a variety of sizes and colors and require very basic conditions. The most important thing is to make sure that their cage never dries out completely because they must be able to keep their external gills moist in order to breathe.*

Left: *This one of the West Indian hermit crabs,* Coenobite clypeatus, *which is sometimes available through the pet trade. Although it may be difficult to identify the various species, they all require the same conditions.*

Right: *This giant land snail,* Achatina *species, is from Africa. It is one of the easiest exotic pets to care for as it is not fussy regarding food or temperature. Because of their eating habits, there is no point trying to arrange plants in their cage, but you should be able to make an attractive but simple set-up using just logs and rocks.*

European fire salamander (Salamandra salamandra)

KEEPING AMPHIBIANS

Amphibians are small vertebrates that usually spend the first stage of their lives in water. This aquatic larval stage is popularly known as a tadpole and it is worth noting that newts and salamanders, as well as frogs and toads, have tadpoles. A few amphibians skip the tadpole stage altogether and hatch from their eggs as miniature replicas of their parents. This is known as "direct development."

Even adult amphibians are dependent on water because they breathe through their skin - unless it is kept moist, gaseous exchange cannot take place. Amphibians maintain their water balance by living in, or visiting, a moist habitat. If captive amphibians are kept too dry they will die of dehydration sooner or later.

Amphibians can be found in a variety of habitats. A number of them are totally aquatic and hardly, if ever, leave the water. Others spend their entire lives beneath the ground and yet another group live and breed in the crowns of immense rainforest trees. There are even toads that live in deserts, burrowing down to avoid the hottest and driest months and forming a cocoon around themselves to protect them from drying out until it rains again. Altogether, there are about 350 species of newts and salamanders and 3,500 species of frogs and toads. Tropical regions are home to far more species than cooler regions and often have greater concentrations of individuals, too. The origin and habitat of the various species are obviously important when it comes to creating suitable conditions for them in captivity.

Keeping a small collection of amphibians can be like bringing a part of the tropics into your home, especially if you house them in an attractive, well-planted vivarium.

Housing amphibians

Amphibian cages are usually based on glass or plastic aquarium tanks. Very often, a standard aquarium without any modifications will be suitable, say for amphibians that live permanently in water or for tadpoles. For other species, some modifications may be required. These might include a specially designed lid to provide more ventilation - even species from damp and humid environments will not thrive in a stagnant atmosphere. Vivarium lids are available in standard sizes as an alternative to the lids supplied with tanks. They provide more ventilation, often have room for a light fitting and are fitted with a small removable panel for introducing food and water. You can buy plastic cages with well-fitting lids, specially designed for amphibians and other small pets. This is the easiest solution if one of the standard sizes is suitable for your amphibians, but bear in mind that plastic cages become scratched and discolored in time. Glass cages are more attractive, but heavier and more fragile.

Certain amphibians are more specialized. For instance, tree frogs like tall cages so that they can climb. Fortunately, the availability of aquarium sealant has made building these cages fairly simple, but give careful thought to their design. The cage must fit into the available space, but be large enough for the animals, as well as lighting equipment, etc. Keep the requirements of the animals uppermost in your mind. If you do not feel competent enough to build your own all-glass cage, dealers in exotic pets will usually be able to produce a cage built to your specifications or suggest someone who can. Plastic food containers and plant propagators are sometimes useful as temporary cages. Animals that are not doing too well in the main display cage may benefit from being isolated in a small container where you can give them special treatment.

Above: The arrangement will look more natural if the pebbles covering the base of the aquatic area are the same type as those in the land area. Make sure they are perfectly clean before putting them in place. Note how the partition slopes, so that the animals can enter and exit.

Right: Using a jug, pour the water gently into the tank in order not to disturb the pebbles too much. The water level should come to about 0.5in. below the divider. Seal around the edges of the divider with aquarium silicone sealant to prevent the water from seeping through to the land area of the tank.

Above: Place a piece of bark or broken plant pot on the land area to give the frogs somewhere to hide. Plunge pots containing small plants, such as ferns and ivies, into the gravel for decoration.

Above: Floating aquatic plants help to keep the water sweet and diffuse the light. This is Salvinia natans, *a small-leaved floating fern. Leave semi-aquatic plants in their pots for ease of cleaning.*

Below: A well-fitting lid is essential once you have added your frog! Make sure that all lights and other electrical equipment are protected from the water. Follow the manufacturer's instructions.

The "clinical" vivarium

Occasionally, it is necessary to keep amphibians under more hygienic conditions. For example, newly acquired specimens may need to be quarantined before they are added to an existing colony or a batch of young amphibians may be too small at first to be introduced to a densely planted vivarium where they will disappear from view. In these cases, plastic food containers or plastic vivariums are ideal. Paper kitchen towels or foam rubber make a suitable substrate. Cut the foam rubber to shape and line the bottom of the container with it, but do make sure that the material has not been impregnated with potentially harmful chemicals.

Above: Frogs and other amphibians can be housed temporarily in very basic enclosures. This one has water covering about one-third of its floor area and a foam substrate. Rinse out the foam periodically.

Heating the cage

Depending on their origin, amphibians may require additional heating. The system you select will depend, to some extent, on the animals' preferred habitat. Aquatic cages can simply be heated with aquarium heaters and thermostats, which are usually combined in a single unit. Terrestrial amphibians may be heated by means of an under-cage heat pad, but this method only works well if the substrate of the cage is not too deep. The same type of heat pad can be attached to the top or to one of the sides of the vivarium and it may be necessary to link the heat pad to a thermostat. In all cases, be sure to follow the manufacturer's recommendations.

Lighting the cage

Most amphibians are secretive by nature and do not require strong lighting. A single fluorescent tube will be sufficient and, even then, the animals should have plenty of cover to hide in if necessary. On the other hand, if you decide to include living plants in the set-up, these will require a suitable level of lighting. You should choose lighting equipment that produces a reasonably natural type of light, and, if necessary, install a time clock to switch it on and off. Avoid using light bulbs, because they become too hot and may be dangerous when installed in a cage that is to be kept humid.

The aquatic vivarium

Some adult amphibians, and all their larvae, require an aquatic set-up. You can arrange this in much the same way as an aquarium for fish, but there are a few additional points to remember. Firstly, even aquatic species may try to escape, so the aquarium must have a well-fitting lid. Secondly, some species are rather large and clumsy, so do not keep them in an elaborately planted and decorated tank. They will be quite happy with a more basic arrangement, consisting of a layer of aquarium gravel, for instance, and some pieces of driftwood. Restrict plants to species that float on the surface, such as *Salvinia*, and water lettuce,

Pistia. A heater/thermostat may be necessary, depending on the species. Aquariums for small species may benefit from a filter, either an undergravel type or a simple box filter. Larger species may require a power filter or regular water changes. When cleaning out aquatic species, it is better to change a proportion of the water at regular intervals than to change all the water at one time. Do not use water straight from the tap. Allow it to stand overnight, so that additives such as chlorine have a chance to dissipate. Alternatively, use rainwater or bottled mineral water to top up the aquarium.

Humidity levels

The humidity level depends on the volume of water in the cage and the amount of ventilation. It is always better to spray the cage frequently, rather than to rely on poor ventilation to maintain high humidity. In a large vivarium it is sometimes possible to install a system of running water, using a small circulatory pump. This will create a localized area of high humidity that the amphibians can visit at will, and is a very successful way of creating the correct conditions for certain of the more delicate species. When using pumps, it is important to ensure that small frogs or tadpoles do not become sucked into the mechanism. If necessary, protect the inset with a plastic grid to avoid such accidents.

Above: Amphibians from heavily forested areas in the tropics or from cooler regions will feel most at home in a planted vivarium with a substrate of bark chippings or dead leaves.

Right: Do not place the plants directly in the substrate, but leave them in pots and bury these up to their rims. They will be easy to remove or replace at a future date if necessary.

Above: Hide the plant pots by placing one or two pieces of rotting wood across the vivarium in front of the plants. Fill the space around the pots with substrate and sprinkle some around the crowns of the plants for a natural-looking display.

Above: Use moss to fill any gaps between the logs and to retain moisture. Replace the moss as necessary. Be sure to buy it from a reputable supplier - it should not be taken from protected or biologically sensitive areas.

Forest vivarium plants

Epiphytic plants grow attached to other trees, and include a variety of ferns, orchids and bromeliads, or air plants. Attach ferns and orchids to pieces of driftwood or dead branches by wrapping their roots in moss and tying the whole bundle to the wood with thin nylon thread. Attach air plants with silicone sealant. If you spray the plants regularly and incorporate a system of running water into the set-up, both the plants and the amphibians will thrive.

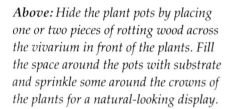

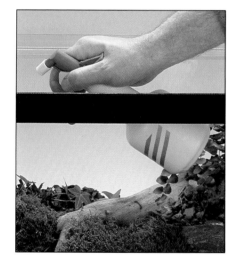

Above: Mist the enclosure using a fine garden sprayer kept solely for this purpose. Label the sprayer to avoid any confusion with sprayers containing pesticides or other dangerous chemicals.

Right: Add the animals; this is a fire salamander. New acquisitions may hide away at first, but slowly become bolder. Many amphibians forage in the evening and this is a good time to feed them.

Feeding amphibians

All adult amphibians are carnivorous. They eat small animals such as insects and worms, although some of the larger species, especially the various types of bullfrogs, will also eat small vertebrates, including other amphibians, small reptiles, and mammals. The tadpoles of salamanders are also predatory, feeding on small aquatic animals, whereas frog and toad tadpoles are mostly herbivorous, eating algae, bacteria, and plants. However, the larvae of some frogs and toads are also predatory.

Feeding adult amphibians should not present any problems as long as you have access to a reliable source of live food. This can be bought or cultured, although breeding your own live food is time consuming and not very cost-effective if the collection is small. A variety of insect species is available commercially.

Crickets form the staple diet of many captive amphibians. Keep them in an escape-proof container until required. They are easier to handle if they are cold so, if possible, put their container into a refrigerator for ten minutes or so before capturing them. Then place them in a small tub and thoroughly dust them with a vitamin supplement containing a high proportion of calcium. This will compensate for the lack of variety that is an inevitable consequence of a captive diet. One problem with crickets and locusts is that if they are not eaten straightaway, they may set up home in the vivarium and damage plants. Chilling the insects before feeding them to the amphibians and only introducing as many as can be eaten at one session are the best precautions.

Mealworms are the larvae of a small brown beetle. They are readily available, but do not constitute a balanced diet if used to the exclusion of all other foods. However, you can offer them in an emergency. Waxworms are the larvae of a small moth that is a serious pest of hive bees. They are very nutritious and highly recommended for salamanders and toads. Feed them to your amphibians as often as possible, but as they tend to be expensive and do not survive well in a damp vivarium, only introduce a few at a time.

Very small amphibians may require a diet of fruit flies, *Drosophila*. These are available as a ready-to-use culture. A few flies will hatch each day until the culture is exhausted, at which

Left: You can collect house spiders and other small invertebrates from around the home and garden to feed to your amphibians, which will benefit from the variation in their diet. However, do make sure that you do not introduce anything too large or dangerous to the amphibian enclosure. For this reason, avoid offering bees and wasps as food.

Right: A Brazilian horned frog, Ceratophrys cornuta, *eating an earthworm. Worms are among the best food for amphibians; if there is a damp area in your garden, it may be possible to collect one or two almost every day of the year. Alternatively, worms are sometimes available from local fishing bait suppliers.*

point it is easier to buy a fresh culture than attempt the messy business of culturing them at home.

Other live foods can be collected from the garden. Many amphibians, especially salamanders and aquatic species, relish earthworms, which are quite easy to find during the spring and summer. Do not waste any spiders, moths, or flies that you find in the home, but make sure that the foods you collect have not been exposed to insecticide sprays, which are lethal to amphibians and other small animals.

Right: Waxworms are the caterpillars of a moth, Galleria. They can be cultured at home, but it is probably easier to buy a small tub when required.

Aquatic newts and salamanders

A number of species of newts and salamanders spend their entire lives in an aquatic environment, while others become aquatic only during their breeding season. All these species need an aquarium, set up according to their size, temperature requirements and so on.

Axolotls

The axolotl is one of the more common species. Axolotls are the larval form of a Mexican salamander that never grows up - it lives its whole life as an overgrown tadpole and even breeds in this state. Although axolotls are now rare in their natural habitat, thousands of them are bred in captivity. They come in two forms, the naturally occurring black form and an albino, or white, form. Axolotls are undemanding pets that tolerate a wide range of conditions. Keeping them at room temperature is usually satisfactory, although their feathery external gills develop more impressively if the water is kept fairly warm - about 73°F is ideal. They need subdued lighting and a diet of small earthworms and other aquatic live foods. A good arrangement for axolotls would be an aquarium with a layer of large pebbles or gravel on the bottom and pieces of driftwood or rocks to provide hiding places. Although it may be possible to grow a few of the more robust

Right: The axolotl, Ambystoma mexicanum, *is named after an Aztec god. It is a larval form of salamander that never metamorphoses, so it can be treated as an aquatic species throughout its life. Axolotls make fascinating and undemanding pets, especially for children, who may not have enough expertise to look after more delicate amphibians. The black and white forms of axolotl are equally suitable for keeping in captivity.*

aquarium plants in a tank containing young specimens, once axolotls reach their adult size of nearly 10in. they are so clumsy that floating plants are a better proposition. A small internal power filter is a good investment, as it will keep the tank clear without the need for large changes of water.

Newts

Other aquatic newts and salamanders require similar conditions but on a smaller scale. The North American and European newts, for instance, spend the spring in ponds and streams and at this time of year the males develop crests on the back and tail. They require a lower temperature than axolotls, say about 54-59°F. After mating, the females lay their eggs singly, carefully wrapping each one in the leaf

Above: The male European smooth newt, Triturus vulgaris, *develops a beautiful crest and brighter coloration in early spring. Other newts undergo similar changes when breeding. Keep them in an aquatic set-up at this time.*

Below: The Japanese fire-bellied newt, Cynops pyrrhogaster, *is an attractive species that will live a long time in captivity if given favorable living conditions. They are often available through importers at very little cost.*

of an aquatic plant. After the breeding season these species will try to leave the water, so move them into a terrestrial vivarium with plenty of places to hide. Feed them on small worms and insects during this phase of their lives.

Good choices of species include any of the European newts in the genus *Triturus* and the Japanese fire-bellied newt, *Cynops pyrrhogaster*. The large European species, the ribbed newt, *Pleurodeles waltl*, is similar in its habits, but is aquatic throughout the year.

The larvae of all newts and salamanders are aquatic, in fact just like miniature axolotls. They require very tiny live foods such as *Daphnia* and, later on, bloodworm. Feed them frequently, otherwise they are inclined to bite chunks out of one another. This is not as serious as it may appear, however, because the wounds heal quickly, provided they do not become infected, and even limbs regenerate.

Terrestrial salamanders

Tailed amphibians living on land are usually known as salamanders. Actually, there is no real difference between newts and salamanders, except this rather arbitrary distinction.

Housing and feeding

Salamanders need a vivarium that is moist and not too warm, with a good selection of hiding places. An aquarium tank with a deep layer of leaf-litter on the bottom and several pieces of bark laid on the surface makes an ideal vivarium. Mossy pieces of wood will enhance the appearance, along with a few potted plants sunk into the leaf-litter. Ivies and ferns are the most appropriate species because they will thrive under the conditions preferred by the salamanders. Spray the vivarium regularly but only lightly - salamanders cannot survive for long in waterlogged conditions. Provide subdued lighting - just enough to keep the plants alive.

An area of water is not essential unless you intend breeding the salamanders. Some species mate and lay their eggs in the water like newts, but the European fire salamander, *Salamandra salamandra*, the most attractive species, mates on the land. Females of this species retain the eggs in their bodies until they are well-grown tadpoles, then sit with their tail and back half of their body in a pool of shallow water and give birth. If a female salamander looks as though she is pregnant, keep a small dish of water in the vivarium so that she can give birth. Make sure the dish has sloping sides and that the water is shallow, otherwise the adults may drown.

Salamanders are especially fond of slugs and earthworms, but some of the more active species will chase and catch crickets and other insects. They quickly become tame and learn to associate their owner with food, emerging in the evening to wait for a meal. Long-term captives may well become overweight for this reason!

Species of interest

The best species to keep are the fire salamander and the North American tiger salamander. Both occur in a variety of forms, all differing slightly in their coloration and the arrangement of their markings. The Chinese mandarin salamander, *Tylotriton verrucosus*, is another attractive species. As long as it is kept in a terrestrial vivarium, it is long-lived in captivity; specimens are often sold as newts, but rarely survive long in a completely aquatic environment.

Some of the smaller North American salamanders, such as the beautiful red spring salamander, *Pseudotriton ruber*, are delicate and difficult to keep alive for any length of time. They require cool flowing water and a deep layer of moss in which to hide. These species are best left to experts.

Below: The spotted form of the fire salamander, Salamandra salamandra, *from Central Europe is the form most often seen in captivity. The bright colors warn predators that the salamander can produce a toxic substance from its skin.*

Right: The striped form of the fire salamander comes from a number of mountain ranges in Europe. All forms make good pets, provided they are kept in a cool place. They have been known to live for over 20 years in captivity.

Toads

Toads differ from frogs in being drier to the touch, warty, and less inclined to leap. Like newts and salamanders, there is no real scientific difference between them and the words "frog" and "toad" are often interchangeable. Toads belonging to the genus *Bufo* are sometimes known as "typical toads." A large number of species are recognized and they are found in almost every tropical, subtropical, and temperate part of the world. These toads are not particularly demanding and make good pets, provided they are given a few basic essentials and are well fed.

Housing
A vivarium for toads should have a deep layer of bark chippings or leaf-litter. Sand and gravel are suitable for the larger species or for species from desert areas. Provide hiding places in the form of bark, logs, or broken clay flowerpots. Large pieces of driftwood with attractive and convoluted shapes are an ideal form of decoration.

Above: The southern toad, Bufo terrestris, *is one of several North American species that are easy to keep in captivity. Toads have a more placid temperament than frogs and usually make more responsive pets.*

Right: The marine, or cane, toad, Bufo marinus, *is the largest of the commonly kept species and will quickly reach hand-sized proportions. It lives a long time in captivity, but needs tropical temperatures and somewhere to hide.*

Right: The red-spotted toad, Bufo punctatus, *is a small, attractively marked species that comes from dry parts of the American Southwest, where it is rarely seen except during summer rainstorms. In captivity it needs a substrate of sandy soil and some flat rocks to hide beneath. It feeds mainly at night on a variety of livefood.*

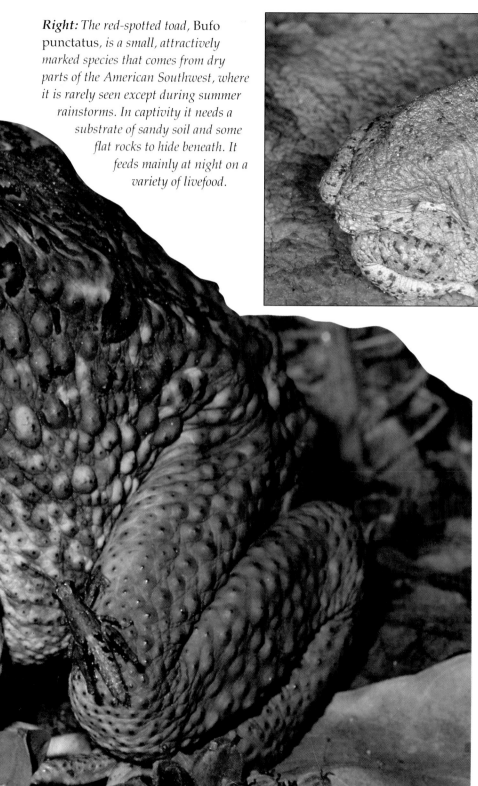

Living plants will survive in a vivarium for smaller toads, but large toad species usually destroy plants in the course of their burrowing activities, unless the plants are left in their pots and protected with large stones around the rim. It is not essential to have a water bowl in the vivarium, but you should spray the enclosure regularly.

If heating is necessary, then an under-cage heat pad is ideal. The temperature at which toads are kept will depend largely on where they come from - tropical species obviously require warm conditions maintained at a constant temperature of about 77-83°F. Although toads prefer subdued lighting, a single fluorescent light will help to keep the cage bright and attractive and may be necessary to keep the plants healthy, especially if the enclosure is situated in a dark part of the room. The light can be controlled automatically with a time switch.

Species of interest

The most common tropical species is the marine, or cane, toad, *Bufo marinus*, originally from South America but also introduced into many other parts of the tropical world. This large species grows to nearly 8in. long and adults will eat other frogs and toads, as well as a variety of the larger insect species. It makes a good pet and soon finds a suitable place in the vivarium where it will invariably be found, patiently sitting and waiting for its next meal. Other tropical species are sometimes imported from Southeast Asia and Africa. These require similar conditions, although none of them grow as large as the cane toad.

Species from the southern parts of North America and from southern Europe also like warm conditions, but will not object if the temperature falls a few degrees at night or during the winter. They rarely require additional heating if kept in a normally heated room in the house. There is a huge variety of species from these regions and almost any of them may crop up in pet stores or on dealers' price lists from time to time. Some of the more attractive species include the western toad, *Bufo boreas*, the southern toad, *Bufo terrestris*, and the red-spotted toad, *Bufo punctatus*, both from western North America, and the green toad, *Bufo viridis*, from southeastern Europe, but there are plenty of others to choose from.

Fire-bellied toads

A number of the many species of toad found throughout the world have become popular pets. These include the fire-bellied toads, especially a species from Southeast Asia known as the Oriental fire-bellied toad, *Bombina orientalis*. It grows to about 2in. long and is most beautifully colored. Its back is bright green with black spots and blotches, while its underside is brilliant red, also with black markings. This species, and the other fire-bellied toads, spend more time in the water than many other species. They need a semi-aquatic vivarium with about 4in. of water and a dry area of gravel and pieces of bark. Floating plants can be grown in the water to good effect. The Oriental fire-bellied toad prefers a temperature of about 68-77°F, so place a heat pad underneath the vivarium. Other species, such as the European fire-bellied and yellow-bellied toads, can tolerate cooler conditions and should not require any supplementary heating at all. Fire-bellied toads spend much of their time floating just beneath the surface with only their snouts and eyes showing. When they see food in the form of small insects, they lunge for it, sometimes using their forelimbs to stuff it into their mouths.

Spadefoot toads

Other groups of toads include the spadefoot toads, found in Europe and North America. The American species live in dry regions, even in the deserts of southwestern USA and Texas. They avoid the driest times of the year by burrowing beneath the surface and producing a cocoon of shed skins around their body, thus protecting themselves from drying out. During rainstorms, they dig to the surface to feed and to spawn in temporary bodies of water.

All these species are quite easy to keep in captivity. They require a deep layer of sandy soil and some flat pieces of rock or bark to hide under. They will burrow to some extent but, provided their enclosure is sprayed occasionally, they will not form a cocoon. Spadefoot toads require a temperature of about 68-77°F and a diet of insects, such as large crickets, locusts, and cockroaches.

Left: *The Oriental fire-bellied toad,* Bombina orientalis, *is almost unbelievably colorful. It makes a good pet if given warm conditions and a large aquatic area. This species will often breed in captivity. Males have thicker forearms than females.*

Right: Scaphiopus couchi, *Couch's spadefoot toad, is the most colorful of the American spadefoots. Although it burrows beneath the surface, it will come out at night to hunt for insects.*

Below: *The Asian horned toad,* Megophrys nasuta, *is related to the spadefoot toads but does not burrow. Instead, it relies on its amazingly leaflike shape and coloration to escape its predators. It makes a splendid and spectacular exhibit when kept in an enclosure with a layer of dead leaves on the bottom.*

Tree frogs

Tree frogs are generally small species, with sticky disks on the end of each toe to help them cling to leaves and branches as they climb. Many are bright green in color in order to camouflage themselves among the foliage, but others are brown. They are at their most active in the evening.

Housing

Tree frogs require a tall vivarium; an adapted fish tank is not very appropriate and most collectors prefer to design and make their own tree frog enclosure, using glass and silicone aquarium sealant. A structure measuring about 24x24x36in. high is ideal for a group of six to ten small tree frogs or for a pair of the larger tropical species. Furnish it with plenty of twiggy branches and some living plants if possible. Houseplants with large shiny leaves look especially attractive. Heat an enclosure for tropical species to about 77-83°F using a heat pad. Attach it to the back or the lid of the vivarium to ensure that all parts receive enough heat, but remember that living plants will not thrive if they are too close to it. If the vivarium is thoroughly sprayed every day there is no need for a water bowl. Alternatively, divide the base of the enclosure with a strip of glass to form a permanent aquatic area. If you opt for this arrangement, make sure you can remove the front of the cage to change the water.

Feeding

Although tree frogs will eat small locusts and crickets, flies are also a good food for them, as they bring out their acrobatic talents. The flies can be hatched out from maggots obtained from bait stores. A few pupae placed in a plastic cup will hatch in about one week. To prevent any flies escaping, put the cup in a refrigerator to chill the flies before introducing them into the vivarium. Dust each batch of live food with a good vitamin and mineral supplement to ensure that the frogs receive a balanced diet. Whenever possible, give tree frogs a variety of natural food in the form of spiders, moths, etc., captured around the house.

Species of interest

A number of species are available from time to time. The common American green tree frog, *Hyla cinerea*, makes a good pet. As it comes from Florida, treat it as though it were tropical and house it in a warm enclosure. Other American species include the gray tree frog, *Hyla versicolor*, and the barking tree frog, *Hyla gratiosa*, which both make good vivarium subjects. The European green tree frogs, *Hyla*

arborea and *Hyla meridionalis*, are also good choices and it is sometimes possible to buy captive-bred specimens of both species. However, beware of the Cuban tree frog, *Osteopilus septentrionalis*: it is very hardy in captivity but will eat smaller frogs and requires solitary confinement!

Other groups of tree frogs come from Asia and Australia. The most common Asian tree frog is the so-called "golden" tree frog, although it is actually light brown in color. This species is very hardy and will thrive under most conditions as long as it is not allowed to become too cold. Of the Australian species, White's tree frog, *Litoria caerulea*, is the species most often encountered. It is a large, plump tree frog that soon becomes tame in captivity. It requires stout branches on which to climb and prefers conditions that are rather

Below: White's tree frog, Litoria caerulea, *is a common species from Australasia. Some individuals can become so tame that they will take food from your fingers, so there is a real danger of overfeeding them! They like a well-lit vivarium.*

Below: The American green tree frog, Hyla cinerea, *is surely one of the most elegant amphibians. It is very common, both in the wild and in the pet trade. It requires warm, humid conditions and, as it is an active tree frog, be sure to provide it with a large enclosure.*

Left: The Mediterranean tree frog, Hyla meridionalis, *makes a tough and long-lived pet. Like most tree frogs, it prefers a tall enclosure, with plenty of branches and some leafy vegetation in which to hide itself away.*

Above: The spring peeper, Hyla crucifer, *is a familiar North American tree frog. It thrives in captivity under fairly simple conditions and appreciates a plentiful supply of small insects, including flies and small moths.*

drier than those recommended for the other species. Offer it a regular supply of large insects. Some individuals even learn to take food from their owner's hand.

The red-eyed tree frog is a very exotic species from Central America. It requires a large vivarium furnished with leafy tropical plants, such as *Philodendron* species. A running water system suits it very well and it makes a most spectacular exhibit when properly displayed. During the day it rests with its eyes tightly closed, but in the evening, when it becomes active, the brilliant red eyes are its most distinctive feature. Red-eyed tree frogs are occasionally bred in captivity and the young frogs may be available through specialist dealers. However, wild-caught specimens can be difficult to acclimatize and are not recommended for beginners.

Bullfrogs

A number of species of frogs from around the world are commonly known as bullfrogs. Although these species are not necessarily closely related, they have many characteristics in common, both in terms of their natural history and their care in captivity, so it is convenient to deal with them collectively.

The most frequently seen species are the South American horned frogs belonging to the genus *Ceratophrys*. Of these, Bell's horned frog, *C. ornata*, is probably the most common, but another species, *C. cranwelli*, is also seen occasionally. In addition, these two species are often hybridized. Horned frogs are remarkable creatures: their mouths stretch right around their huge bony heads, their bodies are almost spherical, and their legs are so short that they appear to have evolved as an afterthought, serving merely to transport the frog from one meal to the next. Above their eyes are the two short fleshy horns that give them their common name. Bell's horned frog is the more colorful of the two species, but both make good pets.

Budgett's frog, *Lepidobatrachus laevis*, and the dwarf Budgett's frog, *L. llanensis*, are similar species from further south, in Argentina. They are equally rotund and have an equally cavernous mouth - with an appetite to match - and are just as easy to cater for in captivity. They lack the horns over the eyes and are more-or-less uniformly gray in color. These two species are also hybridized by commercial amphibian breeders and the resulting offspring are rather tougher than either of the parent species.

In southern Africa, *Pyxicephalus adspersus* is known as the bullfrog. This huge frog is dull green above and dirty white beneath, with yellow areas at the bases of its limbs. Juveniles are mottled in green and brown and have a light stripe running down the body.

Recently, an Australian species has appeared on the scene to complete the bullfrog "team." This is *Cyclorana novaehollandiae*, also known as the water-holding frog. It is less "dumpy" than the other species and rather more agile. It has a more pointed snout and varies in color from light brown to bright green.

All the above species occupy similar niches in their respective habitats. They all live in regions where rainy periods alternate with periods of drought and their defense against dehydration consists of forming a protective cocoon of several layers of skin around themselves and burrowing down into the ground. There they remain for up to several months until the rainy season comes around again. Then they cast off their outer layer and make their way to the surface to feed, breed, and build up food reserves until their next enforced period of "suspended animation."

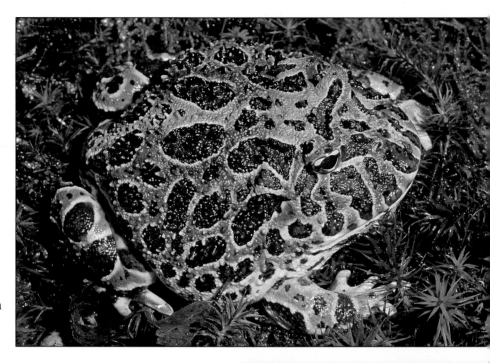

Above: A horned frog belonging to the genus Ceratophrys, *possibly a hybrid. These fantastic frogs make wonderful pets if well cared for. They are produced commercially in large numbers, thus reducing the drain on wild populations.*

Right: Dwarf Budgett's frogs, Lepidobatrachus llanensis, *from Argentina are growing in popularity. They are related to the horned frogs and, although not as colorful, they have the same enormous appetites!*

Housing

In captivity, of course, it is not essential to allow these frogs to dry out. Indeed, it could be dangerous, because they may be unable to take their usual precautions against desiccation. The simplest way to keep any of these species is in a plastic or glass vivarium with a thin layer of rounded pebbles on the bottom. Cover these with a little water. The depth of the water will depend on the size of the frogs - it should be just deep enough to come about halfway up their bodies. None of the species are particularly good swimmers - they are hardly built for it - and deep water is unsuitable. An alternative arrangement is to cut a thick piece of foam rubber to fit into about half of the vivarium and then add water up to the level of the top

A species to avoid

Although it is the "original" bullfrog, the North American species, *Rana catesbeiana*, does not make as good a pet as any of the other bullfrogs. It is very nervous and active and able to jump many feet. This often results in the bullfrog damaging its snout when it is confined to a glass vivarium.

Left: The South African bullfrog, Pyxicephalus adspersus, *is Africa's answer to the horned frogs but a little bigger. It is equally robust and makes a very responsive pet, although some specimens can be rather aggressive.*

Below: The water-holding frog, Cyclorana novaehollandiae, *comes from northern Australia. It is a new introduction to the pet trade and little is known about it, although it seems to be an especially hardy species.*

surface of the foam. If you choose this method, make absolutely sure that the foam has not been treated with chemicals, such as substances designed to retard fire.

Although bullfrogs are not too demanding regarding temperature, try to keep them at 77-80°F by placing a small heat pad controlled by an electronic thermostat underneath the vivarium.

Feeding

All the species mentioned here will eat most live prey, including crickets, locusts, and spiders. As they grow, it may be possible to feed them on small mice that have been stored in the freezer and well thawed before use. Hold the food in front of the frog with a pair of blunt forceps. Wriggling the food around will usually stimulate the frog to lunge for the prey. It should hardly be necessary to add that, because of their attitude to food, it is not possible to keep any of these bullfrog species together. Even individuals of the same species should be kept separately.

Poison dart frogs and mantellas

This section deals with two groups of frogs that, although superficially very similar in appearance and behavior, are not related and are found thousands of miles from one another.

Poison dart frogs come from South America. Their skin contains poisonous toxins as a defense against predators. In order to advertise this fact, they are brilliantly colored and most active during the day. The mantellas, on the other hand, are from Madagascar. They use a similar defense and are also brightly colored. Both species require similar care.

Frogs of this kind are not really suitable for the absolute beginner. They are rarely imported and, although they are not delicate, they have very specialized requirements. However, groups of experienced and dedicated enthusiasts keep and breed these living jewels very successfully. They have such a following that specialist societies have even been formed to share information and encourage successful breeding, thus ensuring a good supply of animals for the future.

Housing
By far the most successful method of maintaining these groups of frogs is in a large planted vivarium with a system of running water. Cover the back of the vivarium with cork or bark and put a layer of leaf-litter on the floor. Add some pieces of dead wood and attach epiphytic plants, especially orchids and bromeliads, to them and to

Handling poison dart frogs

Do not handle poison dart frogs unless it is absolutely necessary. Not only are they small, delicate and easily damaged, but they also produce powerful toxins from glands in their skin. Although these toxins are not dangerous unless swallowed, it is much safer to move the frogs by encouraging them to hop into a small plastic tub. If necessary, cover the tub with a lid while cleaning the frogs' vivarium or while moving them to another vivarium. If you must handle the frogs, be sure to wash your hands thoroughly afterwards and keep all equipment, etc., well away from foodstuffs.

the back of the vivarium. If the lighting is adequate to encourage the healthy growth of the plants, it will also be the right intensity for the frogs. Two or three fluorescent lights, preferably the kind that simulate natural daylight, should be sufficient. Aim to keep the temperature at about 73-83°F for poison dart frogs, but mantellas prefer slightly cooler conditions; in fact, they often thrive at room temperature in a normally heated room.

Feeding
Because these frogs are small, their food must be carefully graded. Fruit flies are the most suitable diet for young frogs and for adults of some of the smaller species. Larger frogs will tackle small crickets, but be sure to chill these before introducing them to the vivarium, because if any escape from the frogs, they will wreak havoc among any growing plants. It is equally important to dust each batch of live food with a good vitamin and mineral supplement, preferably one containing a high proportion of calcium. Despite their size, all these frogs have large appetites. Feeding them once each day is not really enough; if possible, try to introduce food two or three times every day, especially in the case of young frogs.

Left: This mantella, Mantella madagascariensis, *has appeared under a variety of names. However, one thing is certain: it is among the most beautiful of Madagascan species and is sure to remain popular with keepers as long as stocks are available.*

Right: Dendrobates tinctorius *is known as the dyeing poison dart frog because pigments from its skin have been used to dye feathers and clothes. It fares well in captivity and is bred in quite large numbers in Europe and North America.*

Species of interest

Very many species are included in these two groups and all require similar conditions. Some are extremely difficult to maintain, while others are somewhat easier. Restrict your early attempts at keeping a group of these frogs to the more straightforward species, such as the tricolored poison dart frog, *Epipedobates tricolor*, the dyeing poison dart frog, *Dendrobates tinctorius*, the green-and-black poison dart frog, *D. auratus*, the golden mantella, *Mantella aurantiaca*, and the Madagascan mantella, *M. madagascariensis*. In general, mantellas are rather easier to keep than poison dart frogs. There should be plenty of scope here to get a feel for these beautiful frogs before you move on to the more demanding species.

Above: Epipedobates tricolor *is from Ecuador. It is recommended as a good species for beginners, as it will live and breed under a variety of conditions; many of the other poison dart frogs are rather more demanding.*

Right: *The blue poison dart frog,* Dendrobates azureus, *is arguably the most beautiful amphibian. Its fabulous coloration sets it apart from all other species but, unfortunately, it is rare and somewhat delicate in captivity.*

Protecting poison dart frogs

Some species of poison dart frogs have very small natural ranges, sometimes just a few hundred square yards. All natural populations are protected under CITES - the Convention on International Trade in Endangered Species. All poison dart frogs offered for sale should have been bred in captivity. At the time of writing, such restrictions do not apply to the mantellas, but it seems likely that they will also be protected in the near future.

Aquarium frogs

A small number of frogs are totally aquatic. These species, all from South America and Africa, are all in one family and range in size from about 1.2 to 6in. Aquarium shops sometimes stock the smallest species, *Hymenochirus* sp., or "dwarf aquatic frogs." They come from Africa and are easy to care for. House them in an aquarium heated to 73-77°F and control the temperature with an aquarium heater/thermostat. Install an undergravel filter and cover the bottom of the tank with a layer of fine aquarium gravel. The aquarium should be thickly planted with species such as *Vallisneria*, and some twisted pieces of driftwood will enhance its appearance, as well as giving the frogs somewhere to hide. Grow floating plants, especially *Salvinia*, on the surface so that the frogs can hide among the trailing roots. These small frogs will eat any of the live foods sold for fish, especially *Daphnia* and bloodworm. They sometimes eat flaked fish food but offer this sparingly, as it will turn the water cloudy if too much remains uneaten.

Although it is possible to keep fish with the frogs, do not include any aggressive species that may bully or damage the frogs. On the other hand, the frogs will happily gobble up any baby fish, such as guppies, if they are present.

Clawed toads

Other aquatic frogs are larger. There are several species of African clawed toad belonging to the genus *Xenopus*, and they are definitely not good companions for fish. They have hearty appetites and large mouths and will systematically reduce the fish community as they grow. They are also rather boisterous and soon uproot delicate plants. Driftwood, floating plants and, perhaps, one or two larger aquarium plants firmly tucked away behind rocks are the best forms of decoration. Clawed frogs require a similar temperature to dwarf aquatic frogs and an efficient filter to keep their aquarium reasonably clean. They will eat earthworms and almost any other live food, either dropped into the water or floating on the surface. In an emergency they can be fed on strips of lean meat, but this does not make a satisfactory long-term diet for them.

Right: *The African clawed frog,* Xenopus laevis, *is easy to care for under very basic conditions. You can keep these frogs in a simply furnished aquarium with about 6in. of water and they will wait just below the surface for food to arrive. Feeding can be a rather hectic affair! You can offer them food, such as worms, on the end of a pair of long tweezers, but make sure there are no sharp edges on which the frogs may damage themselves.*

Above: The dwarf clawed frog, Hymenochirus boetgeri, *is often offered for sale by tropical fish dealers. It prefers to be kept with its own kind, rather than with fish, however, and will* feel most at home in an aquarium with subdued lighting and some old roots or pieces of driftwood amongst which to hide. These frogs are most entertaining when kept together in a small group.

The Surinam toad

The most bizarre of the aquatic frog species is the Surinam toad, *Pipa pipa*, sometimes known simply as the pipa toad. This South American species grows to 6in. long or more, has an extremely flattened body, tiny eyes, huge hind feet, and small front feet. Each of its fingers ends in a small star-shaped structure that appears to be sensitive to movement in the water. Surinam toads are remarkable for carrying their eggs and tadpoles on their back throughout their whole development, only releasing them after they have metamorphosed into tiny toadlets.

The care of this species is broadly similar to that of the others, but rooted plants stand little chance in the aquarium. However, large pieces of driftwood are ideal; attaching some Java moss, *Vesicularia dubyana*, to them will create a natural and most attractive effect. Surinam toads prefer to eat small fish, but in the absence of these they will accept larger types of live food, such as earthworms, and can sometimes be trained to accept crickets and locusts from the surface. Although these are fascinating animals to keep, it is a good idea to gain some experience with commoner species before attempting to keep them.

Fat-tailed gecko (Hemitheconyx caudicinctus)

KEEPING REPTILES

Reptiles form one of the major orders of animals, dating back to the time when dinosaurs and other prehistoric creatures ruled the earth. Living species number about 6,500, with more being discovered every year in remote parts of the world.

Reptiles differ from amphibians in having scaly bodies and, more importantly, in laying shelled eggs or giving birth to live young. It is this feature that has made them so successful, allowing them to colonize areas where there is little water and thus exploit a whole new range of habitats. Although only a very few reptile species are suitable, or available, for captivity, they form a fascinating cross-section of animals. Many of them are beautiful, others are impressive, all are interesting.

The reptiles are split into several groupings. These are the chelonians (turtles and tortoises), the crocodilians (crocodiles and alligators), the tuatara, a strange survivor from prehistoric times, the lizards, and the snakes. We will confine ourselves to members of those groups that make good pets, namely the lizards, snakes, turtles, and tortoises.

Reptiles show a greater range of sizes than either of the other main groups discussed in this book. This is bound to be a consideration when choosing which species to buy and keep. Not many people have the facilities to house fully grown pythons or giant tortoises, for example. Remember this when selecting your reptile and also bear in mind that even the largest species start out small. Is that 3ft.-long snake you are thinking of buying a fully grown ratsnake or a newly hatched python that will eventually outgrow your home and threaten the safety of other pets and children?

Housing reptiles

Many of the enclosures described for amphibians are also suitable for housing reptiles. As before, the requirements of the animals must take priority over aesthetic considerations. However, there is still plenty of scope for arranging attractive cages, especially if you choose to keep the smaller species. The size and shape of the cage should reflect the habits of the species housed in it. For example, arboreal reptiles require tall cages, whereas active terrestrial reptiles require plenty of floor space. Most creatures will require cages with lids, but small ground-dwelling species are often unable to climb smooth surfaces and can be kept in open cages, provided there is no danger from other pets, small children, etc.

Heating the cage

The key to keeping reptiles successfully lies with meeting their temperature requirements. All reptiles are ectothermic, which means that they rely on an outside source of heat to keep their body temperatures at a suitable level. If this is not available, they cease feeding, become lethargic and susceptible to disease and eventually die. In the wild, they regulate their body temperatures by living in warm climates, basking in the sun and hibernating during cold weather if necessary. In captivity, they only have a limited opportunity to carry out these activities, so it is vital that you are aware of their temperature requirements.

Each species has an ideal body temperature that it will try to maintain at all times. In general, reptiles operate most efficiently at temperatures ranging from 68 to 95°F, depending on species. The exact preferred body temperature may vary from night to day and from summer to winter, so it is impossible to arrive at a satisfactory value that will suit all the species all of the time. The answer to this problem is to give each reptile a choice of temperatures, so that it can choose where it wants to be at any given time.

For this reason, it is a good idea to situate all heating equipment, whether it be heat pads, light bulbs or more powerful ceramic heaters, towards one end of the cage. The occupants can then choose to sit close to the heater or move away to a cooler part of the cage. Take care when positioning thermostats; if the thermostat is situated in the warmest part of the cage, set it at the highest temperature suitable for the reptile, whereas if it is in the coolest part of the cage, set it at the lowest appropriate temperature. Keep a thermometer in the cage at all times so that you can check the temperature.

Above: Leaving them in their pots, add some small plants that require very little water. Arrange them in one or two groupings for the maximum effect.

Above: A heat pad and thermostat have been installed under the tank. Now add a free-running type of sand with a fairly natural coloration - builder's sand is not usually suitable. Burrowing species require a layer of several inches, but a shallow layer will suit surface dwellers.

Left: An old log or, better still, a cactus skeleton, will hide the pots. More than one piece may be needed for larger cages. Anchor them firmly into place.

Above: Complete this naturalistic set-up with a few large pieces of rockwork, plus some similar-looking smaller chippings around the plant pots.

Plants for dry enclosures, such as for desert lizards

Cacti, e.g. *Gymnocalycium* and *Mammillaria*	Small-growing, barrel-shaped species
Aloe spp.	Succulent members of the lily family from Africa and Madagascar
Haworthia spp.	Similar to smaller versions of *Aloe* spp., also from southern Africa
Crassula, Sedum and *Kalanchoe* spp.	Many undemanding species available from garden centers. They often survive where more specialized succulents fail.

Lizards, turtles, and tortoises

As a rule, lizards and turtles prefer higher temperatures than snakes. Many of these species like to bask in a very warm area, known as a "hot-spot," which you can create by focusing a spotlight or ceramic heater onto a rock or branch on which the reptiles can rest. Hot-spots should only be available during daylight hours. At other times, create a suitable background temperature using under-cage heating and a thermostat to ensure that the cage does not overheat.

To sum up, a basic set-up for lizards, turtles, and tortoises should consist of a roughly rectangular cage with a heat pad underneath and a spotlight at one end to produce a hot-spot during the day. During the day, the reptiles will shuttle back and forth, keeping their body temperatures within their preferred range.

Snakes

Snakes' preferred body temperatures tend to be lower than those of other reptiles and, except for a few species, they rarely bask in the open. A basic set-up for snakes should consist of a cage with a heat pad under one end only, applying heat to between one quarter and a half of the floor area. Additional heating is not necessary and any lights should be of the fluorescent variety that give out little heat. The temperature setting of the cage will depend on the species to some extent, but because the animals can move about to choose their own temperature, precise control is not necessary.

Above: Direct a small spotlight onto the rocks, but not the plants, and turn it on for at least eight hours every day. The lizards will bask in the hot-spot.

Above: A fat-tailed gecko is introduced to its new cage. It soon settles in and learns to come to the front of the cage when offered food by its keeper.

Below: The completed cage will offer an insight into the lives of these fascinating animals. Routine maintenance involves cleaning the sand regularly, watering the plants, and checking that electrical equipment is working effectively.

Decorating the enclosure

Most reptiles do not need an elaborately decorated cage and are quite content with somewhere to warm up, somewhere to cool off, and somewhere to hide. On the other hand, an attractively laid out vivarium looks more natural, complements the animals, and helps to keep them interesting.

The first point to remember is that if you want an elaborately arranged cage you will have to reject certain species straightaway, including all the large snakes and most of the small and medium-sized ones as well. Similarly, large lizards, turtles, and tortoises will do everything in their power to wreck any attempts to make their surroundings aesthetically pleasing. The best you can do with large reptiles such as these is to incorporate a substrate that is not too unsightly and put one or two heavy logs or rocks in the cage. Suitable substrates include bark chippings or wood shavings. Gravel and any kind of soil are totally unsuitable. Newspaper makes an effective but unattractive substrate for large species. Alternative beddings, such as granulated corn cob and ground walnut shells, have been tried out on lizards and snakes with some success. These materials look attractive, are light in weight, and are easily replaced when soiled, but they are fairly expensive in the long term.

Above: A thin layer of gravel is the best substrate for most aquatic reptiles. Use a type that looks natural with no sharp edges. Wash it well, but do not use chemical cleaners or disinfectants.

The naturalistic approach

Maintaining a naturalistic cage can be time-consuming but very rewarding. Plants may need pruning or replacing and areas of the substrate may have to be replaced occasionally. The glass front and sides of the cage will need frequent cleaning, as will water bowls and, possibly, lighting tubes. Try to rearrange the furnishings of the cage as little as possible, so that the reptiles can establish regular basking and resting sites. The naturalistic approach works best with small lizards that can be given a substrate in keeping with their natural habitat.

Creating a forest environment

Forest reptiles include several climbing geckos such as the day geckos, small anolis lizards and other spectacular species, such as the chameleons. Again, small species will do less damage in a delicately arranged cage than larger ones, which tend to be clumsy.

Plants for a forest vivarium, such as for climbing lizards

Ficus spp., e.g. *F. benjamina*, the weeping fig and its varieties, and *F. natalensis*	Tropical figs suitable for tall cages
Philodendron, especially *P. scandens*, the sweetheart vine	Grows over dead branches
Anthurium spp., flamingo plants	Some will grow over dead branches, cork bark, etc.
Spathifolium spp., peace lilies	Prefer rather damp conditions

All these species climb and their cages can look especially attractive if they are thoughtfully decorated. The substrate can consist of bark chippings or leaf-litter. Arrange a selection of interesting pieces of dead branches for the lizards to climb and perch on, and then add one or two living plants. Many houseplants are suitable, but choose robust species with sturdy stems and branches so that the animals can clamber about in them without doing too much damage. Tropical figs, *Ficus* species, are popular houseplants and well suited to tall lizard cages. Alternatively, try climbing plants trained to scale the dead branches already installed. Remember that some lizards eat vegetation - there is no point in giving them expensive houseplants to consume - and that crickets and locusts intended as food can be equally destructive if you introduce too many to the cage at a time.

As a last resort, you can buy some very good plastic plants. Although these rarely look totally natural, they do give the reptiles something to climb over and hide in. The plants can be removed and washed if necessary, but do not require any other attention. Furthermore, they do not get eaten!

Above: Firmly attach a combined heater/thermostat to the back of the tank. If possible, slope the unit slightly so that the thermostat portion is higher than the heating element. Make sure that the unit is a fully submersible one.

Above: A small power filter keeps the water clear. This one can be installed inside the tank and attached by rubber suction pads. Large, messy reptiles require a more powerful, external power filter or frequent cleaning by hand.

Creating a desert environment

Desert species should have a layer of sand or gravel covering the bottom of the cage, but try to avoid builder's sand or gravel, which looks totally unnatural and may contain harmful salts and impurities. Aquarium gravel rarely looks correct either, but is a good standby. The best source of natural material is the countryside, but make sure that there are no restrictions on collecting such material and, in any case, take it from an inconspicuous place. Avoid material that may be contaminated with oil or chemicals. Try to collect a few larger rocks of the same material as the sand or gravel so that when the cage is landscaped it will look as though you have recreated a small area from a desert. Some stores stock short sections of cactus "skeletons" and these can really enhance the look of a small desert set-up if used with care.

There are plenty of desert plants for sale, especially cacti and succulents. To be authentic, you should only use cacti in cages containing American desert species and succulents for reptiles from elsewhere. These plants need very little water, but an enormous amount of light. If the cages are not brightly lit, the plants will become drawn, i.e. they will turn pale green and bend towards the light. The only remedy is to remove the plants and place them in a more suitable spot until they recover. This task is made easier if you keep the plants in small pots buried to the rim in the substrate. You can then remove and replace them as necessary.

Below: Monitor the temperature and quality of the water for two or three days before introducing any animals. Give your new pet a few hours to acclimatize before offering it any food.

Above: Driftwood makes good basking sites for turtles and will not rot. Place pieces directly beneath a spotlight suspended well above the water level. Plastic plants are a good choice in a tank housing boisterous, active species.

Right: After you have arranged the gravel, equipment, and decorations, pour the water in gently. Tapwater or rainwater is normally suitable for aquatic reptiles - pond or stream water may contain harmful parasites.

Feeding reptiles

When it comes to food, reptiles fall into three main categories: strict herbivores that only eat vegetable material; strict carnivores that only eat animal material; and omnivores that eat some of each. Some species' diets change as they grow, so that the young, for instance, eat mainly insects, but the adults eat mainly plants.

Herbivorous species include the green iguana and all land tortoises. They require a good selection of vegetable material, including green leaves, fruit, and root vegetables. If necessary, you can chop their food into small pieces and mix it thoroughly. You may find that certain individuals have preferences and sort through the food to get at the items they like best - if this results in waste, modify the mixture accordingly. Sprinkle a liberal amount of vitamin and mineral supplement over all feeds.

Carnivorous reptiles range from small lizards, such as the geckos that eat insects, to large boas and pythons that consume mammals the size of rabbits or larger. Insectivorous species usually only eat food that is alive. In most parts of the world, live crickets, locusts, mealworms, and waxworms are available from specialist dealers,

Ultraviolet light and vitamin D_3

Many lizards, turtles, and tortoises - but not snakes - require an artificial source of ultraviolet light when they are denied access to natural sunlight, as in captivity. They need this in order to produce Vitamin D_3 which, in turn, is important in the conversion of calcium into bone, shell, etc. Without ultraviolet light, these species develop skeletal deformities and soft shells and their lifespan is reduced.

There are two kinds of light fitting on the market that produce ultraviolet rays. One is a natural spectrum tube that produces some UV light along with the other parts of the spectrum. The other type gives out UV but very little other light. These fittings are known as blacklights and are the most effective way of providing the necessary amount of UV light. Unfortunately, they do have one drawback - they produce an eerie bluish glow! However, you can counteract this by installing a normal warm white fluorescent tube alongside the blacklight. Blacklights are normally available through specialist dealers in reptiles and equipment. They can be left on all day, although the animals should be able to move away and into shade if they wish.

Left: A common boa, Boa constrictor, makes short work of a dead rat. Snakes have an amazing capacity to stretch their mouths and eat relatively large meals. They do not need daily feeding.

Below: Two tropical tortoises enjoying lettuce leaves. They will need a variety of vegetables and fruit, supplemented with vitamins and minerals, if they are to remain healthy in the long term.

Left: Insectivorous lizards, such as the bearded dragon, Pogona vitticeps, *require daily feeding. Experience will tell you how many insects to give them each time. Some individuals develop dietary preferences, but try to ensure that they all get a good variety of food.*

Right: Mealworms are the larvae of a beetle, Tenebrio molitor. *Although they are a convenient food and are readily available by mail order from specialist dealers, they lack several important minerals and vitamins. For this reason, you should only use them very sparingly.*

either locally or by mail order. In addition, you can collect insects with a sweep net, as long as there is no danger of introducing pesticides or other noxious chemicals along with them. Dust all insect food with a vitamin and mineral supplement.

Reptile dealers normally supply rodents intended as food in a frozen form, so train snakes and large lizards to accept food items that have been stored in the freezer and thawed out as required. Rodents are a complete diet and reptiles fed on them require no extra vitamins or minerals. Some carnivorous lizards will eat canned dog and cat food. This is convenient, but do not offer them too much, as this type of food usually contains a great deal of protein and not enough roughage, resulting in obese animals.

Newcomers to the reptile-keeping hobby may be confused over how much and how often to feed their pets. As a rule, herbivorous species should be fed every day, although they will not come to any harm if they go one or two days without food every now and again. If they leave large quantities of food, you are probably overfeeding them, so reduce the quantity and give them one day each week without food. On the other hand, if they pounce on their food and consume it all within a few minutes, they are probably underfed, so gradually increase the amount of food until they seem more satisfied. A well-fed reptile will look sleek, with a well-rounded body and limbs.

Insectivorous species also require daily feeding but, again, will come to no harm if they miss the odd day or two. Species that eat larger prey, such as rodents, will only require occasional feeding. Young snakes and lizards may accept a small mouse or rat every three or four days, but as they grow, offer them larger but less frequent meals. By the time they are adult, one or two prey items

every 10-14 days will be sufficient. Breeding females are the exception to this rule: they require feeding twice as often.

Reptiles' appetites often vary according to the time of the year. In the winter they may eat less than during the summer, even if they are kept warm by artificial means, so adjust their feeding accordingly. Reptiles that are cooled off in the winter, perhaps in preparation for breeding, will not require feeding at all, but fresh drinking water should be available at all times.

Food supplements for reptiles

No matter how great a variety of food you offer captive reptiles, they will always lack certain elements present in their natural diets. In particular, diets for captive reptiles tend to contain too much phosphorus and not enough calcium. The problem can only be corrected by adding a mineral supplement to their food. The most useful supplements are those containing a high proportion of calcium; good-quality products will list their ingredients on the box or tub.

Another way of boosting reptiles' calcium intake is to give them cuttlefish "bone" as fed to budgerigars. This is especially beneficial for young tortoises; if necessary, you can grate the cuttlefish over their food. Young turtles will bite pieces out of a large chunk floated in their water.

Female geckos also benefit from cuttlefish, because their hard-shelled eggs contain a great deal of calcium. They will deliberately eat small pieces of cuttlefish placed in their cage and store the calcium in special sacs on either side of the throat.

Ground geckos

Various species of ground-dwelling geckos are found throughout the world, many of them in deserts and other arid habitats. Most of them like to burrow, but have only limited climbing ability. For this reason, they are fairly easy to house in low enclosures with a substrate of sand or grit and a jumble of rocks to hide in. One or two succulent plants in pots plunged into the sand or grit will add interest to the vivarium.

Heat the enclosure using a heat pad placed under one end and maintain the temperature at about 68-77°F during the day, but slightly lower during the night. Lights are not strictly necessary, as these lizards are mainly nocturnal, coming out of their retreats during the evening to hunt for food. However, lighting will improve the appearance of the vivarium and will be essential if plants are included. Ultraviolet lights are not necessary for this type of lizard.

Feeding

All ground geckos eat insects and a balanced diet can consist of crickets, locust hoppers, waxworms, and small insects found in the garden. Liberally dust all food with a vitamin and mineral supplement. Females that are forming eggs will require extra calcium in the form of small slivers of cuttlefish bone placed in a dish in the cage. Drinking water should always be available and it is a good idea to lightly spray one area of the cage every day, as a little localized humidity will help the geckos to shed their skins more easily when the time comes.

Species of interest

A variety of species is available. By far the best known is the leopard gecko, *Eublepharus macularius*, from Pakistan. This species grows to about 6in. long and has a swollen tail when it is well cared for. It is widely bred in captivity and babies can usually be obtained throughout the spring and summer. This lizard is the ideal starter reptile. The fat-tailed gecko, *Hemitheconyx caudicinctus*, is closely related to the leopard gecko but comes from Africa. It is slightly larger but requires similar conditions. Other species include the banded gecko, *Coleonyx variegatus*, from North America, several species in the genera *Paraoedura* from Madagascar, and *Stenodactylus* from North Africa and the Middle East. All these geckos can be treated in much the same way, but do not mix the species. Males are territorial and aggressive, so house only one male in each enclosure.

Left: The leopard gecko, Eublepharus macularius, *is the perfect first lizard. It is easy to care for, becomes quite tame and will even breed in captivity, provided it is kept warm and well fed. Babies are boldly banded at first and take about one year to reach adult size.*

Right: The fat-tailed gecko, Hemitheconyx caudicinctus, *is an African species, closely related to the leopard gecko. It, too, is a rewarding pet, although not as common at present. Both species eat a wide variety of live insect prey. Females of both species lay a pair of soft-shelled eggs, which must be kept in damp sand or vermiculite if they are to hatch. Other geckos lay hard-shelled eggs, like those of birds, and these can be kept drier, with just an occasional spray.*

Right: Stenodactylus petrii *is a species of sand gecko from North Africa. All sand geckos are very small - less than 3in. in total length - but they make interesting pets. A small group requires* a natural-looking vivarium set-up, with sand as the substrate and a jumble of small stones and rocks to hide amongst. These active burrowers only appear on the surface of the sand in the evening.

Determining the sex of ground geckos

Ground geckos such as the leopard gecko, as well as several other lizards, turtles, and crocodilians, do not have the usual X and Y chromosomes that determine the sexes in mammals and most other reptiles.

When the eggs are laid, the developing embryo does not have a sex. However, by the time the eggs hatch, the young gecko will be either male or female. What happens between egg-laying and hatching depends on the temperature at which the eggs are incubated. Although the eggs are viable over a range of temperatures, those that are relatively cool can only develop into females, whereas those that are relatively warm will develop into males. The exact temperatures depend on the species, but in the leopard gecko, for example, temperatures below 84°F produce females, whereas temperatures above 88°F produce males. Temperatures in between may produce either sex.

In turtles and crocodiles, the system works in reverse - low temperatures produce males and higher temperatures produce female offspring.

Climbing geckos

Of the 800 or so species of geckos found throughout the world, most are characterized by small "sticky" pads on the tips of each of their toes. In fact, the pads are not sticky, but consist of millions of small hooks that attach themselves to any small irregularity in the surface. These climbing geckos can even run up glass or hang upside down on ceilings. In tropical countries, many of them live alongside man, running around at night inside houses, restaurants, and hotels, hoping to catch insects attracted by the lights.

Housing and feeding

Not surprisingly, their climbing ability makes these geckos rather difficult to accommodate. Enclosures must be totally escape-proof and you must take great care when opening them for spraying, feeding, and so on. If you provide plenty of hiding places at the back of the cage, the geckos will be more likely to hide than to try and escape whenever you open their cage.

The ideal enclosure for a small group of climbing geckos would be a tall glass cage with a removable front for occasional thorough cleaning, and a smaller opening in the top for spraying and for introducing food on a day-to-day basis. You can cover the back with cork bark or cork tiles attached with aquarium sealant and arrange a number of dead branches or sections of cork bark so that the geckos can creep behind them.

Cover the bottom of the cage with sand or fine gravel. A layer of dead leaves may be more appropriate for forest species. A water bowl will complete the set-up; if there are breeding females in the enclosure, include a small bowl to hold pieces of cuttlefish bone. A temperature of 68-77°F is suitable for almost all species, even though they are found in various parts of the world.

Climbing geckos eat any kind of active insect, including crickets and locust hoppers. Flies are a good food, as they tend to accumulate around the top of the cage, where the geckos spend much of their time. Dust every meal with a good vitamin and mineral supplement, but there is no need to provide an ultraviolet light.

Right: The tokay gecko, Gekko gecko, comes from Southeast Asia. It is one of the largest species in the family and its bright coloration makes it a popular species with hobbyists. It is easy to care for under tropical conditions, but be warned - this species can give a painful bite. Its name comes from its loud call "To-Kay," and most geckos vocalize to some degree. Bear in mind that as a rule, geckos dislike being handled and should be disturbed as little as possible. They frequently discard their tails if they are handled too roughly.

Species of interest

There are very many species to choose from and not all are correctly identified when they appear in pet shops. The largest species is the tokay gecko from Asia, a spectacular, if bad-tempered, species requiring a large cage. Many of the smaller species go under the name of "house gecko" and are often gray or brown in color with blotches and lines on their bodies. The "flying" geckos from Southeast Asia are remarkable for the flaps of skin along their flanks and the webbing on their feet, which enable them to glide from tall trees. All these species have similar requirements and are easy to keep under captive conditions.

Left: The West African long-tailed gecko, Tropiaclotis *species, grows to about 3.2in. Over half of this is the tail, which is easily detached. Provide a warm, humid vivarium (78-85°F daytime temperature), with plenty of branches, hiding places, and a small water bowl. This nocturnal species feeds mainly on small spiders, aphids, and small crickets. It lives for 6 to 8 years.*

Above: The Asian house gecko, Hemidactylus frenatus frenatus, *is common and widespread, often found near human dwellings, where it hunts for flies and other pests. It is easy to keep in captivity, but a secure cage is essential for this fast-moving gecko.*

Below: The bronze gecko from the Seychelles, Aeluronyx seychellensis, *is an interesting species with an unusual means of defense: if you try to hold it, its skin will come away in your hand, leaving an ugly pink area. For this reason, you should never handle it.*

Day geckos

Most geckos are nocturnal, but a few species are active during the day. Many of these are brightly colored by comparison with the grays and browns of the nocturnal species. The day geckos of the Indian Ocean are placed in the genus *Phelsuma* and there are about 23 species altogether.

With one or two exceptions, these geckos are bright green or greenish blue, with a variety of markings on their heads and bodies. Some are quite large, notably *Phelsuma madagascariensis*, of which a number of different forms are recognized. This species grows to almost 12in. long. The smaller species are all about half this size and are often a better choice for the home vivarium, as a small group can be kept together in an attractively planted enclosure.

Housing

All the day geckos have pads on their toes and are, therefore, a subdivision of the climbing geckos described on pages 84-85. All the precautions regarding escape-proof enclosures apply equally to day geckos, and their diet and temperature requirements are also similar.

Day geckos require tall cages with plenty of vertical surfaces to climb and rest on. Stout lengths of bamboo are very suitable and females often lay their eggs inside the hollow sections. Other appropriate decor includes plants such as *Yucca*, with its thick trunk and tufts of leaves sprouting from the top and sides, or small palms.

Above: Standing's day gecko, Phelsuma standingi, *is one of the more showy species - specimens in good condition are bright blue-green. Male day geckos of any of the species should not be kept together, as they will fight fiercely, and large species such as this can inflict serious injuries on one another as a result.*

Left: Abbott's day gecko, Phelsuma abbotti, *although not as bright as many species, is subtly marked and easily tamed. This species does not appear in pet stores very often, but a number of similar species are available from time to time. Their care is the same regardless of species.*

The lighting will need to be quite bright if such plants are to thrive. Day geckos seem to require a certain amount of ultraviolet light, so install a natural spectrum tube or, better still, a blacklight alongside the light required by the plants.

Day geckos should be sprayed occasionally, but do not allow their enclosure to become too humid. A good plan is to use potted plants and to keep the compost moist at all times, so that when the geckos require a little extra humidity, say when they are about to shed their skin, they can find a suitable spot in which to spend some time.

Male day geckos are very territorial and females also react badly if they are overcrowded. A small community therefore needs plenty of room and, in particular, several suitable perches and hiding places so that the geckos can space themselves out.

A temperature of about 77°F suits day geckos very well and they will come to no harm if this falls slightly at night. They eat all the usual insect food, but dust each meal well with a vitamin and mineral supplement. In addition, they seem to enjoy licking at sweet substances (in nature they often drink nectar from tropical flowers). In captivity, they will find a sugar cube, laced with a few drops of a liquid multivitamin preparation, quite irresistible and will gradually lick it away to nothing. They also relish honey or the artificial nectar sold for certain tropical birds; all these items add variety to the diet.

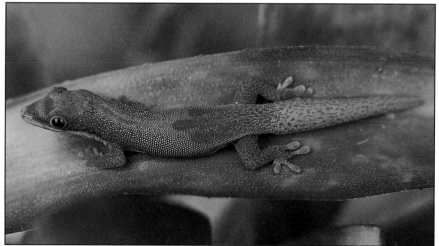

Left: Phelsuma madagascariensis *is often known as the giant day gecko. It grows to 12in. or more and occurs in a variety of color forms, all of which are beautiful. This species requires a large vivarium with plenty of living plants to climb about on. It will also eat larger insects than other species.*

Above: *The gold-dust day gecko,* Phelsuma laticauda, *belongs to a group of smaller species. These are more suitable for hobbyists with limited space, as a pair will be content with a cage measuring about 40in. in all dimensions This species is especially fond of nectar, honey, or sugar.*

Iguanas

The iguana family contains a few large lizards and a great number of small species. Many of them are brightly colored, active species that make interesting displays. All require a warm, spacious vivarium with a spotlight to create a hot-spot during the day and a powerful ultraviolet light if they are to thrive.

The green, or common, iguana

The green iguana epitomizes the tropical rainforest and is a popular pet. Although this species does not breed readily in captivity, it is farmed commercially in parts of Central America and babies are frequently available. Newly hatched youngsters are bright green and measure about 12in., but the tail accounts for over half of this. However, by the time they are fully grown, they can measure well over 39in. and weigh many times more than the hatchlings.

Housing

One or two young green iguanas will live in an enclosure measuring about 40x20x20in. high. Provide a spotlight with a branch immediately below it, so that the lizards can bask at will. Iguanas also require an ultraviolet light, preferably a blacklight. As they are tropical lizards, maintain a background temperature of at least 68°F at all times. During the day, the iguanas should be able to raise their body temperatures to 86°F by basking under the spotlight. Adult iguanas need a proportionately large cage, with sturdy branches for basking. Because iguanas are herbivorous, you cannot put living plants in the enclosure, but plastic plants can be used to good advantage. Aquarium gravel, bark chippings or newspaper all make suitable substrates that are easy to change when necessary.

Green iguanas are normally kept individually, otherwise they may fight. Handling tame iguanas should not present any

Right: The common iguana, Iguana iguana, *is a popular species with pet stores. You should buy a young specimen if possible, as it will adapt better to captivity. In addition, young iguanas are easier to handle and to house, although you will have to provide a roomy enclosure equipped with an ultraviolet light if they are to grow into healthy adult specimens.*

Below: Adult green iguanas may grow to over 5ft. long. Keeping them in suitable accommodation is a serious undertaking. Many keepers like to allow their iguana out of its enclosure, at least for part of each day, and it usually finds a perch high up in the room or conservatory where it habitually rests. Make sure that the iguana cannot escape or come to any harm.

great difficulties, but nervous specimens are not so easy; they can inflict painful scratches with their claws and also use their long tails as a whip. The most sensible plan is to buy the iguana when it is a baby and handle it carefully and regularly from the start.

Feeding

Green iguanas are herbivorous and eat a range of leaves, flowers, fruit, and vegetables. Offer them a good variety of food, preferably chopped up and well mixed so that they cannot select just a few favorite items. Always add vitamins and minerals to their food. Some individuals have strange tastes and keepers sometimes find that their pet will go to any lengths to obtain leftover cooked vegetables or even jelly sandwiches, for example! Juveniles sometimes eat insects as well as vegetation and you can give them a few crickets or mealworms occasionally. Fresh drinking water must be available at all times and iguanas seem to enjoy a thorough spraying once or twice a day.

Below: *The plumed basilisk,* Basiliscus plumifrons, *a showy South American iguanid, can sometimes be found in the more specialized pet stores. All basilisks are fast-moving lizards that require a spacious enclosure.*

Right: *Species such as the helmeted iguana,* Corytophanes cristatus, *are related to the green iguana, but need a diet of insects rather than vegetation. In general, you are likely to find them more demanding in captivity.*

Other species of interest

One or two other large iguana-like lizards may be kept in the same way as green iguanas, but they rarely have the same appeal. The basilisks, for example, of which there are several species, are attractive, but rather nervous in captivity. Unlike green iguanas, they eat insects. Similarly, the spiny-tailed iguanas, *Ctenosaura* species, from Mexico, rarely grow completely tame and require a huge vivarium if they are to be at all happy in captivity.

The North American desert iguana and chuckwalla are desert species that need a large, but not necessarily tall, enclosure. Instead of branches, give them a pile of rocks to bask on and make sure that the temperature under their spotlight is very high - at least 104°F. These species are herbivorous and feed on a similar range of plant material as the green iguana.

Smaller iguana species

Not all iguanas are large, dragonlike lizards. Very many smaller species come from a variety of habitats, including humid forests, deserts and mountain ranges throughout North, Central and South America. Although not as impressive, they can make interesting pets and have the added advantage that a small group can be housed together in an attractively arranged enclosure.

Anolis lizards

The anolis lizards are small tropical and subtropical iguanids. The green anolis, for example, is found in the warmer states of the USA. It is a good climber and rarely found on the ground. It is bright green in color, although it may change to brown at times. Males have a pink, fan-shaped dewlap that they flick up and down during sessions of display, either to other males or to females. The brown, or Cuban, anolis is brown and cream, with an orange dewlap. Both these species are frequently sold in pet shops, along with a larger species, the knight anolis.

Housing and feeding

Anolis lizards require a subtropical vivarium heated to about 86°F under the spotlight during the day, and with a background temperature of 68-77°F. They also need ultraviolet light, which can be installed alongside a normal, white fluorescent tube. Provide a tall enclosure with plenty of vertically arranged branches and tall living plants if possible. They also like fairly humid conditions, so spray the enclosure daily, but make sure it is well ventilated so that the atmosphere inside does not become too steamy. All the anolis lizards eat insects, including crickets and flies. They derive great benefit from food collected from outside and are especially fond of spiders. Dust every meal with vitamin and mineral powder.

Below: The green anolis, Anolis carolinensis, *is sometimes called the American chameleon. It can change color from green to brown in the space of a few minutes. Do not confuse it with the true chameleons, however, which all come from Africa or Madagascar.*

Iguanids to avoid

A number of medium-sized iguanids are definitely **not** suitable for community cages. These are the collared lizards, *Crotaphytus*, and the leopard lizard, *Gambelia*. All the lizards in these genera specialize in eating smaller lizards, so there is no chance of housing them with other species. In captivity, they will also eat large insects such as adult locusts. In any case, collared and leopard lizards are rather difficult to keep successfully because they require very large enclosures with powerful spotlights and plenty of ultraviolet light.

Left: The brown anolis, Anolis sagrei, *originates in Cuba but has been introduced into Florida, where it is often seen in parks and gardens. It makes a good pet. The males have bright orange throat fans, which they erect when they display to one another.*

Right: A wide variety of lava lizards, Leiolaemus *species, were imported from Chile until recently. Now the trade is restricted but a number of small species are still available. Some are egg-layers, others give birth to live young.*

Below: Fence lizards, such as this Sceloporus occidentalis, *are common over much of North America and make lively and attractive pets. A small group in a well-arranged vivarium will give much enjoyment, but make sure that there are enough hiding and basking places for each of them.*

Spiny lizards

Other small iguanids include the spiny lizards of the genus *Sceloporus* from North America, some of which are also known as fence lizards or swifts, and several closely related species, such as the side-blotched lizard and the brush lizards. These active species do quite well in captivity as long as they have an ultraviolet light, a hot-spot and plenty of small insects. They require drier conditions than the anolis lizards and rocks or dead cactus skeletons make appropriate cage furnishings.

Lava lizards

From South America there is a huge range of small iguanids known collectively as lava lizards. Most belong to the genus *Leiolaemus* and it is often difficult to identify them exactly. Although they are similar in appearance to the North American spiny lizards, they come from high mountain habitats and require hot days and cold nights if they are to thrive in captivity. Their diet consists of insects and other small invertebrates.

Setting up a community

When choosing a group of small iguanids for a vivarium, whatever the species, it is important not to pick just the brightly colored individuals. These will almost certainly be males and a number of males in one cage will fight each other until only one or two dominant individuals remain. The best arrangement is to select one male - the brightest and healthiest-looking specimen - and one or two females. This will lead to a more harmonious community.

It may be possible to include individuals of more than one species in a community cage but this can be rather risky. Some species do not react well if others are present and, in addition, they may require slightly different conditions. Finally, some species may turn out to be more efficient hunters and monopolize the food supply.

Dragon lizards

Lizards belonging to the family agamidae are often known as "dragons." Although there is a large number of lizards in this family, including some spectacular ones, only a few are easy to keep in captivity. Agamid lizards like very hot conditions and must have access to a source of ultraviolet light. If either of these are missing, they will not survive.

Bearded dragons

Bearded dragons, from Australia, are undoubtedly the best choice, especially for beginners. There are several species, all in the genus *Pogona*, but as there are only slight differences between them and their care in captivity is similar, they can be dealt with together. Bearded dragons reach a length of 12in. or so, half of which is tail. Their common name comes from their habit of puffing out their throat when they are angry or excited. This raises a patch of pointed scales, making them stand on end like a beard or ruff.

Young bearded dragons are blotched with dark gray markings on a lighter background, but as they grow these markings become less distinct. They do not have "beards"; these develop as they mature. Some specimens develop yellow or orange markings on the head and front half of the body and in others, mainly males, the throat becomes black, especially when they are excited or displaying to one another.

Housing and feeding

Bearded dragons require large cages with a hot spot and some dead branches on which to perch and bask. Aim for a daytime temperature of 86-104°F beneath the hot spot, but at night the temperature can fall to 68-77°F or even less without the lizards coming to harm. Bearded dragons raised in captivity become very tame and will take food from their owner's hand. They especially like large insects, such as locusts and crickets, but will also eat vegetable

Left: The bearded dragon, Pogona vitticeps, *will become a very tame pet if obtained as a juvenile (shown here). It has an enormous appetite and eats most insects, but encourage it to accept fruit and leafy vegetables as well.*

Below: The beautiful Thai water dragon, Physignathus concincinus, *is a semi-aquatic dragon from Southeast Asia. Look for healthy specimens - many freshly imported water dragons are in poor condition by the time they reach the pet stores.*

Right:
Adult bearded dragons, Pogona vitticeps, *are not as brightly marked as the juveniles. They make up for this in personality, however, and will readily take food from their keeper's hand - especially if you offer them an item they are particularly fond of, such as a large locust or mealworm. Many owners like to give their pet the run of the living room for a few hours each day. If you decide to do this, make absolutely sure that the animal cannot harm itself or effect an escape.*

material, including watercress, dandelion leaves and flowers, and salads. Dust each meal with a vitamin and mineral supplement, otherwise the lizards' skeletons will not develop properly.

Breeding
The difference between the sexes is not great and babies, in particular, all look the same. If you hope to breed bearded dragons, the best method of obtaining a pair is to buy three or four babies and hope for the best. As they mature, males will become dominant and can usually be identified from their behavior. Provided the cage is large enough, two or more males that have been raised together will live together fairly peacefully, but new males introduced to an established colony may be attacked. Females are not territorial and it is possible to keep several together.

Other species of interest
Other species of agamid lizards are sometimes offered for sale, but many of these are not suitable for keeping in a small vivarium. Water dragons and sailfin lizards, for instance, are spectacular but nervous creatures, and often damage their snouts when they panic as a result of disturbance. Captive-bred babies are sometimes available; if you have enough room to build a large vivarium, measuring at least 78x78x39in. high, they will settle down well.

Chameleons

Chameleons are arguably the most fascinating of all lizards. They have several unique features, of which their ability to change color is but one - and often exaggerated at that! In keeping with their arboreal habits, all chameleons have a prehensile tail that is often coiled like a watch spring when not being used to grasp a branch. The toes are fused into two groups and opposed to one another, so that they act as pincers, again for grasping branches, and the body is greatly flattened from side to side so that they can balance more easily. Their camouflage is legendary - apart from looking rather like a green leaf, chameleons enhance this deception by moving very slowly and swaying from side to side as they go.

When it comes to feeding, they have two other unique adaptations. Their eyes rotate independently of one another, so that a hunting chameleon can stalk its prey and keep a wary eye open for predators at the same time. Only when it is about to reach for its prey do both eyes focus on the same point for a second or so. Then the chameleon demonstrates its final "trick" - the tongue can be extended a huge distance, often equivalent to the length of its body, and ends in a sticky tip so that the prey is knocked off its perch and withdrawn into the chameleon's mouth in one swift operation.

Choosing a suitable species

With such an array of bizarre qualities, it is no surprise that chameleons are high on the list of potential reptile "pets." Unfortunately, keeping them alive for any length of time is by no means easy. Most begin to fade away almost as soon as they are removed from the wild and die shortly after importation. With care, however, one or two species can be kept - and even bred successfully - in a vivarium. **The secret is to choose the right species.** So far, the Yemen species, *Chamaeleo calyptratus*, has proved the most successful. This large and impressive chameleon seems to adapt to captivity rather well. The panther chameleon, *C. pardalis*, from Madagascar also thrives under the right conditions, while a smaller species, *C. lateralis*, also from Madagascar, has also been kept with some degree of success.

Caring for chameleons

Having selected a suitable species, there are several other points to remember. Firstly, it is essential to provide chameleons with a source of ultraviolet light. A blacklight or natural spectrum light must be fitted inside their cage and left on for at least eight hours every day. Secondly, chameleons eat enormous quantities of food - a couple of young *Chamaeleo calyptratus*, for instance, can easily dispose of 50 small crickets each day! Furthermore, every feed must be well dusted with a vitamin and mineral supplement and the cage should be sprayed with water every day, as chameleons have great difficulty in drinking from a water bowl.

The final point to bear in mind is that chameleons are very antisocial lizards. Males will not tolerate each other in the same cage or even if they can see one another through a glass divider. Even females are not too happy about sharing their cages with other individuals. A large cage could contain a male and a female, or possibly one male and two females, but attempts to keep large groups together are almost certainly doomed to failure - the lizards will become stressed, refuse to feed and eventually waste away. It is important, therefore to be able to tell the sexes apart if you are thinking of keeping more than one chameleon. Usually, this is not too difficult with the adults, although juveniles can look similar to one another. As a rule, male chameleons are more brightly colored than females of the same species and, if the species is one with horns or crests, those of the male will be larger and more extravagant.

Housing

Apart from the advice given above, an enclosure for chameleons is no different from that of any other arboreal lizard. The cage should be tall and furnished with a network of twigs and branches so that the animals can get about. One or two living pot plants will greatly improve the enclosure's appearance and will give the lizards somewhere to hide and surfaces from which to drink drops of water. It is not necessary to provide high temperatures for most species of chameleons - 72-83°F is quite adequate - and it will not be harmful if this falls slightly at night.

Above: An African species, the sailfin chameleon, Chamaeleo montium, *is sometimes seen in captivity. Like many chameleons, though, it is very difficult to care for properly and you should leave this species to the experts.*

Right: The Yemen chameleon, Chamaeleo calyptratus, *is an exception to the rule - this species copes very well with life in captivity. It is large and colorful and will probably become more easily available in future.*

Skinks

The skink family contains over 2,000 species and occurs throughout the warmer parts of the world. Most skinks are small, with smooth, shiny scales and a pointed snout. These lizards tend to live secretive lives beneath leaf-litter and other debris and are rarely seen, even in places where they are common. In captivity, they make good vivarium subjects because they are undemanding and do not usually need specialized diets or equipment. Although some of them are rather drab in color, they are alert and lively lizards and there is always something happening in an enclosure containing a small group of them.

Blue-tongued skink

The choice of species is very wide. Among the more popular are the Australasian skinks belonging to the genus *Tiliqua*, sometimes known as blue-tongued skinks. These are larger than other members of the family, growing to about 12in. long and heavily built. Most of the members of this group will eat canned dog or cat food, as well as insects, dead mice and some vegetation. Although an ultraviolet light is not essential, specimens will be livelier if there is one available. Otherwise, all they require is a gravel or sand substrate, a water bowl and pieces of bark or broken flowerpot to hide under.

Above: The five-lined skink, Eumeces fasciatus, *belongs to a group of attractive North American skinks that can be kept quite easily in captivity. Although they dislike being handled, they quickly learn to recognize their owner and will wait eagerly for small insects to be placed into their cage. Spray this species' cage occasionally.*

Left: There are several species of blue-tongued skinks from Australasia, of which this species, Tiliqua gigas, *from New Guinea, is the most common. All species are easily catered for and make amusing, long-lived pets. Being slow-moving, this species can easily be handled and will become quite tame. All blue-tongued skinks are live-bearing, producing up to 25 youngsters.*

Stump-tailed skink

The stump-tailed skink, a very distinctive member of the family, looks more like a double-ended fir cone than a lizard. It does very well in captivity under the same conditions as the blue-tongued skinks, but is hard to find and very expensive to buy.

Mediterranean eyed skink

There are literally hundreds of smaller skinks to choose from. Species from hot, dry places, such as the Mediterranean eyed skink, require a medium-sized vivarium with a heat pad under one end and a spotlight focused on a rock or dead branch. Provide a sand or fine gravel substrate and somewhere for the lizards to hide - a piece of cork bark is ideal. Mediterranean eyed skins relish crickets, mealworms, and other insects. This species and several other skinks give birth to live young; about five or six relatively large babies are born in spring or early summer and are quite easy to raise.

Five-lined skink

Other skinks are more at home in a forest environment. Several of the North American skinks, such as the five-lined skink, for instance, require rather moister conditions. A layer of leaf-litter or bark chippings makes a good substrate, with pieces of bark laid flat for the skinks to hide beneath. Maintain the temperature at about 77°F in summer, but allow it to fall slightly during the winter. These skinks eat crickets and other small insects, and lay eggs. Several forest skinks, including the five-lined species, have bright blue tails as babies, but this coloration tends to disappear as they mature.

Green tree skink

Other colorful species are the green tree skinks from Asia. There are several species, all rather similar in appearance. They require a more humid environment, with branches and plants to climb on and a constant temperature in the region of 68-77°F.

Sand fish

The sand fish, *Scincus scincus*, is a very specialized and interesting species. It normally lives in sand deserts, swimming rapidly through the dunes and only appearing on the surface when it is hunting food. This skink can make a fascinating captive, even though you will rarely see it!

Left: The sand fish, Scincus scincus, *is a most remarkable lizard and shows several adaptations to its unusual lifestyle. In captivity it needs a deep layer of fine sand, a supply of small insects and very little else! If you stick to a regular feeding time, however, it will emerge on schedule every day, pushing its nose out of the sand first of all to check for food.*

Monitors and tegus

Although the monitors and tegus are not related, superficially they are similar and require similar care. All these large and impressive lizards require spacious cages once they are fully grown. Do not buy babies unless you can accommodate them later on. Furthermore, most species never become very tame and can only be handled with difficulty; they use their teeth, claws, and tails to good effect!

Monitors come from Africa, Asia, and Australia. Only a few species are commonly available, namely the water monitor, the bosc's, or rock, monitor, and the Nile monitor. The first two are somewhat easier to tame than the Nile monitor. Tegus come from Central and South America. They sometimes have a calmer temperament, but even so, they can be aggressive and give a painful bite. If you are determined to keep a monitor or a tegu, the best advice is to buy a young specimen and try to tame it before it becomes too large.

Housing and feeding

Creating a naturalistic cage for any of these species is a complete waste of time, as they will quickly destroy any plants and churn up the substrate. The best alternative is a layer of gravel or sand. Newspaper is more convenient because it is easier to change, but it does not look particularly attractive. Place one or two large rocks or logs in the cage for the lizards to climb on and situate one of these underneath a powerful spotlight or heater so that the animals can bask. Maintain the background temperature at a minimum of 68-77°F. The temperature under the spotlight should approach 104°F when it is turned on during the day.

These large dragonlike lizards are meat-eaters and will accept canned dog and cat food, as well as insects, rodents, and eggs. They have large appetites and can become rather obese, so ration their food. Needless to say, they should not be kept with smaller lizards.

Left: The Indian water monitor, Varanus salvator, *is an impressive animal by any standards. Compared with some monitors, this species can become relatively tame, but its huge size - it can attain over 5ft. in length - makes keeping one a serious undertaking. Its cage should be strongly constructed of timber and glass. A large water bowl is essential; as its common name suggests, this lizard likes to soak itself thoroughly.*

Right: *The tegu,* Tupinambis teguixin, *is the South American counterpart of the monitors. This beautiful lizard can also grow very large and requires a correspondingly large cage. A bad-tempered tegu is a force to be reckoned with! You may need the assistance of another person when handling one.* T. rufescens *is a similar species that grows slightly larger. Its care in captivity is identical. Tegus belong to the same family as the familiar American whiptail lizards.*

Large boas and pythons

A large boa or python is often a beginner's first, though not necessarily the best, choice of snake. The species most commonly offered are the common boa, *Boa constrictor*, and the Burmese python, *Python molurus bivittatus*. The reticulated python, *Python reticulatus*, and the African python, *Python sebae*, are also seen from time to time. A fifth species of giant snake, the anaconda, should never even be considered for captivity due to its aggressive nature.

These are impressive snakes and their care in captivity is a serious undertaking. They all attain a relatively huge size, potentially up to about 26ft. in the case of the reticulated python, slightly less for *Python molurus bivittatus* and *Python sebae*, and about 10ft. in the case of the common boa. At these sizes the snakes require large enclosures and equally large items of food. Handling can become a problem, especially if the snake is a bad-tempered individual.

If the lure of a large snake is irresistible, the best choices are the common boa or the Burmese python. They are the smallest of the group and have the most predictable temperaments. In addition, both these species are widely bred in captivity and young specimens are frequently available. These are more likely to adapt successfully to captivity than wild-caught specimens.

Housing and feeding

When they are young, these species can be kept in much the same way as other snakes. However, once they approach adult proportions, the only practical type of accommodation is a large wooden enclosure with a glass front. All-glass enclosures may be feasible if they are built into a corner or an alcove. Heat the enclosure by means of a powerful element firmly fixed to the roof and well protected by a strong metal guard to prevent the snakes from touching it and burning themselves severely. Install a reliable thermostat and maintain the temperature at about 80°F. Provide a substrate of newspaper, which you can cover with wood shavings or even dry leaves for aesthetic purposes. Obtaining appropriate food items can be something of a problem. Rodents, even large rats, are hardly more than a snack for a large Burmese python, for example, so you will have to locate a reliable source of rabbits and/or poultry.

Breeding

Breeding is achieved quite frequently with the common boa and the Burmese python. The fundamental difference in the reproduction of the two species is that whereas the python lays eggs, the boa gives birth to live young. Pythons are unique among snakes in that the females coil around their eggs for the duration of the incubation period. In captivity, the eggs can be left with the female or removed to an artificial incubator. Burmese pythons typically lay about 30 eggs, which hatch after about 60 days incubation. Common boas give birth to litters ranging from 5 to 40 young, depending on the size of the female. Raising the young of either species should not present any problems - except cage space!

Safety first

Even perfectly tame boas and pythons cannot be trusted completely. **Never** wrap a large specimen around your neck and **never, ever** give one to a small child to play with. Large pythons and boas that are given the run of the house are likely to look on other pets - dogs and cats, for example - as meals.

Above: Baby Burmese pythons, Python molurus bivittatus, *are often available, as the species breeds readily in captivity. In addition, there is a yellow (albino) strain, as well as a number of other color variants. Any of these do very well in captivity and will make spectacular and attractive pets. Be forewarned, though, that they can all grow to a potential 15ft. in length and require appropriately sized meals. If this is likely to become a problem, resist the temptation to buy this species and consider a smaller type of snake.*

Below: The common boa, Boa constrictor, is a widespread and variable species. The photograph shows a dwarf form, known as the Hog Island boa, that is more easily accommodated than the mainland boas. It grows to a maximum of about 6ft. long, as opposed to the lengths of 8 or 9ft. that some of the mainland species can attain.

Right: The Amazon tree boa, Corallus enhydris, is a long, slender snake. Juveniles, such as the one pictured here, are attractive and can be kept in a well-planted vivarium but, unfortunately, as they grow older, they often become aggressive and rather difficult to manage. At the same time, they tend to lose their bright coloration.

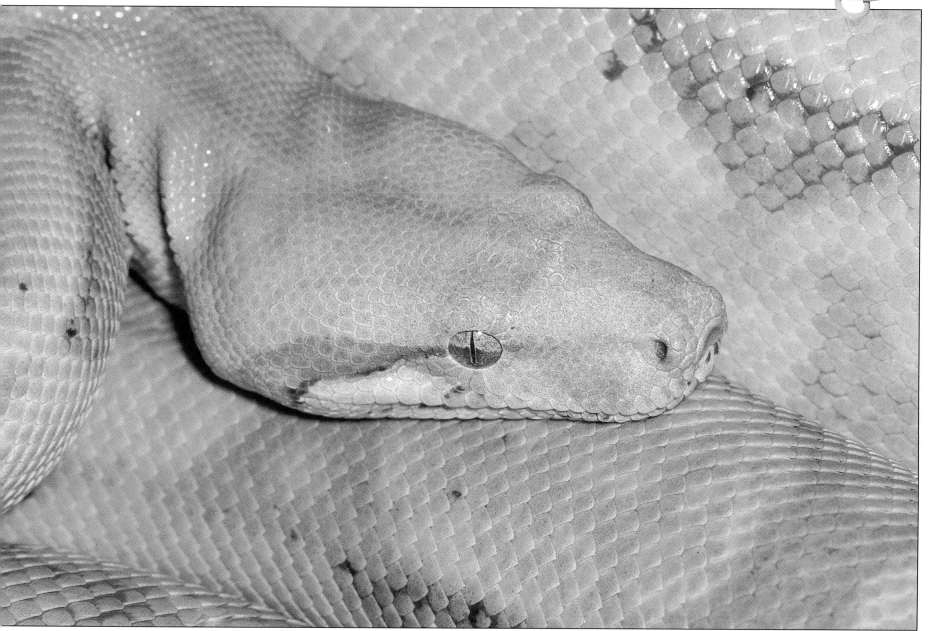

Small boas and pythons

Although they may not be as spectacular as some of their larger relatives, the smaller boas and pythons tend to make better pets. Many of them only grow to a length of 36in. or so and are easier to accommodate in the home. Furthermore, their food requirements are more modest: most species eat mice, although one or two of the larger ones will also accept small rats.

Housing

Small boas and pythons can be housed in a vivarium made of glass or of plastic-coated wood with a glass front. The size will depend on the species to be kept in it, but 36x20x20in. high is sufficient for most of them. However, some species like to climb and they need taller enclosures. Most species are tropical or subtropical and will require a temperature of about 80°F most of the time. In order to give them a choice, place an under-cage heat pad beneath about one-third of the vivarium floor. The most convenient substrate is newspaper covered with softwood shavings. Aquarium gravel is a possible option, but it is heavy and difficult to keep clean. Other furnishings include small boxes or pieces of cork bark to provide hiding places at each end of the cage and, possibly, a branch for the arboreal species to climb on. A bowl of fresh water should be available at all times and this should be large enough for the snake to submerge itself completely.

Below: Rosy boas, Lichanura trivirgata, *only grow to about 36in. long. Their small size and placid nature* makes them ideal pets, although they can be expensive. The photograph shows a specimen from Baja California.

Left: The Brazilian form of the rainbow boa, Epicrates cenchria cenchria, *is a deservedly popular species. Rainbow boas, named for their brilliant iridescence, reach about 6ft. in length and are much more manageable than some of their larger cousins.*

Right: Spotted pythons, Liasis maculosus, *are among the smallest species in their family. Apart from their size, they show all the characteristics of other, larger pythons, including the heat-sensitive pits along their lips and their habit of coiling around their eggs.*

Species of interest

There is a range of species to choose from and it is not possible to mention them all. Rosy boas, *Lichanura trivirgata*, come from North America. There are four or five subspecies, all of which grow to about 36in. long. They are docile and adapt well to captivity.

The rainbow boa grows to about 36-72in. long and is found throughout much of South America. It is divided into several subspecies. The Brazilian form is the most brightly colored. The attractive emerald tree boa, *Corallus canina*, also comes from South America, but this species needs rather more specialized attention than the others.

Moving to Africa, the most frequently seen species is the royal python, *Python regius*, which grows to a little over 36in. This species is imported in large numbers, but wild-caught specimens often fail to adapt to captivity and refuse to feed. Captive-bred snakes are more likely to thrive.

The sand boas are much smaller. They all belong to the genus *Eryx* and are found in East and North Africa and in parts of Asia. The most common species is *Eryx colubrinus*, known as the Egyptian, or Kenyan, sand boa, depending on subspecies. The rough-scaled sand boa, *Eryx conicus*, comes from the Indian subcontinent and is rather larger, growing to about 36in. All the sand boas like to burrow and need a substrate of sand or similar material. Here they will wait in ambush for their food, with just their heads showing.

Finally, a few Australian species are sometimes available. The smallest is the Children's python, *Liasis childreni*, which grows to about 30in. The spotted python is slightly larger at 36in., while the carpet python can sometimes attain 72in. or more. The latter species likes to climb and benefits from a tall cage furnished with some strong branches and an additional heater fixed to the top, so that it can stay warm without sitting on the floor of the cage.

Ratsnakes

The ratsnakes form a popular and attractive group of medium-sized snakes. They are found in North America, Europe, and Asia and most of them belong to the genus *Elaphe*.

The corn, or red, ratsnake
The corn snake is a species of ratsnake and belongs to the same genus, *Elaphe*. It is by far the most popular species and probably the best choice of snake for the beginner. It is divided into two subspecies, *Elaphe guttata guttata*, the corn snake, or red ratsnake, which is the typical and most common form, and *Elaphe guttata emoryi*, known as the plains ratsnake. The latter subspecies lacks the red coloration of the typical form and is thicker and more robust.

   In addition to these two subspecies, there are many different forms of the corn snake. Some are due to geographical variations, but many are the result of chance mutations, which have been further increased by selective breeding. The main, naturally occurring forms are the "Miami" phase, which has a gray background and orange saddles, and the "Carolina" phase, which has deep red saddles, often with a thick black border, on a yellowish or orange background. There are many intermediate forms and most captive-bred corn snakes are difficult to assign to a specific population.

Other forms of interest
Of the various mutations available, the most distinctive ones are those lacking one or more colors. Thus, the "amelanistic" form lacks black pigment and the "anerythrystic" form lacks the red pigment. If both pigments are missing, the snakes are almost pure white with pink eyes and are known as "snow corns." The most attractive

Housing a snake

Below: Most snakes prefer a simple set-up. This can be based around an aquarium, which should be well washed and sealed around the inside corners. Begin by placing a layer of wood shavings or similar material over the floor of the cage.

Above: The snake must have a place to hide in, such as a piece of curved bark or a small wooden or cardboard box.

Right: Provide fresh water at all times. The snake needs to crawl into a bowl to take a soak without causing the bowl to overflow or tip over. Wash the bowl and replace the water every other day.

Above: A well-fitting lid is vital. You can buy vivarium lids from reptile dealers or make one yourself.

Right: Allow the snake plenty of time to explore its new surroundings undisturbed. Some snakes will eat within hours of moving to a new cage; others refuse food for the first few days.

Left: Specimens of corn snake, Elaphe guttata, *from South Carolina are especially sought after for their brilliant coloration, but there are several other attractive forms and variations.*

mutations are bred in large numbers and are freely available from breeders or through the pet trade. One other attractive mutation is not so common at present. This is the "striped" phase, in which the saddles are lacking altogether and the red coloration is "blended" into a pair of stripes running along the back of the snake. These lines are more prominent in juveniles.

Housing, feeding, and taming

The corn snake, in any of its forms, is among the easiest species of snake to keep and breed in captivity. It grows to about 39in. long and is easily accommodated in a medium-sized vivarium measuring, say, 24x12x12in. Provide a temperature of about 68-77°F using a heat pad placed under one end of the cage. Corn snakes feed exclusively on rodents and most individuals will accept defrosted mice of the appropriate size. Hatchling corn snakes eat the smallest size of newborn mice, or "pinkies," and normally take two each week.

Corn snakes are very tame, a factor that makes them an ideal species for the beginner. Handle them carefully when they are small and they will become accustomed to human contact as they grow. Try not to handle them for a day or two after they have been fed, as this can upset their digestions, and never handle them at all when they are about to shed their skin.

Breeding corn snakes and other ratsnakes

Breeding will only take place if you cool the adults for two or three months during the winter. Once they have warmed up in early spring, give the male and female three or four feeds each and then place them together. They will usually mate within a few days and should be separated again some time before the eggs are due. The female may require extra feeding during the early stages of gestation, but when egg-laying is close she will often refuse to feed altogether. About ten days before egg-laying she will shed her skin; now place an egg-laying container, with a layer of peat or moss on the bottom, into her cage. Do not handle her more than necessary at this stage.

A clutch can consist of 6 to 30 eggs, depending on the size and condition of the female. After laying she will be hungry, and will soon make up the weight she has lost. It may be possible to mate her again in order to produce a second clutch, but only attempt this if she is in first-class condition and feeding well. On the other hand, some females lay a second clutch whether or not they are put back with the male.

The eggs hatch after about 70 days; the exact period varies slightly according to the incubation temperature. The hatchlings normally shed their skins about a week after hatching and should begin feeding on the smallest size of newborn mice, soon after. With adequate feeding, they grow quickly; in fact, it is possible to breed corn snakes that are only 18 months old.

Below: The plains ratsnake, Elaphe guttata emoryi, *is a subspecies of corn snake that is not so brightly marked. However, it makes a good pet and is, if anything, even easier to keep than the corn snake. All forms of this species are easy to keep and breed and are trouble-free, provided they are well looked after.*

Other ratsnakes of interest

Several other North American ratsnakes are frequently kept in captivity. These include the various forms of the common ratsnake, *Elaphe obsoleta*, Baird's ratsnake, *Elaphe bairdi*, and the Trans-Pecos ratsnake, *Bogertophis subocularis*. Of the European species, the most attractive one is the leopard snake, *Elaphe situla*. A number of Asian species are available from time to time, including the Taiwan beauty snake, *Elaphe taeniura*, the Indian trinket snake, *Elaphe helenae*, and the Japanese ratsnake, *Elaphe climacophora*. Although several of these occur in more than one form, all make good captives provided they are in good condition when you acquire them. Buy only captive-bred stock, especially where the Asian species are concerned, as wild-caught snakes of these species often harbor parasites.

Housing

Caring for all these species is fairly straightforward, but they do vary in length and the size of their vivarium should reflect this. The largest species, such as *Elaphe taeniura*, can grow to over 72in. and they require a correspondingly large enclosure. Others, such as the European leopard snake, rarely reach even 36in. and can therefore be kept in much smaller accommodation. The species also vary slightly in their temperature requirements according to their origin, but the

Commonly bred species of ratsnake

North American species

Corn snake (red ratsnake)	*Elaphe guttata guttata*
Great plains ratsnake	*Elaphe guttata emoryi*
Black ratsnake	*Elaphe obsoleta obsoleta*
Yellow ratsnake	*Elaphe obsoleta quadrivittata*
Gray ratsnake	*Elaphe obsoleta spiloides*
Everglades ratsnake	*Elaphe obsoleta rossalleni*
Baird's ratsnake	*Elaphe bairdi*
Trans-Pecos ratsnake	*Bogertophis subocularis*

Asian species

Indian trinket snake	*Elaphe helenae*
Taiwan beauty snake	*Elaphe taeniura*
Russian ratsnake	*Elaphe schrenkii*
Redtailed ratsnake	*Gonyosoma oxycephala*

European species

| Leopard snake | *Elaphe situla* |
| Four-lined snake | *Elaphe quatuorlineata* |

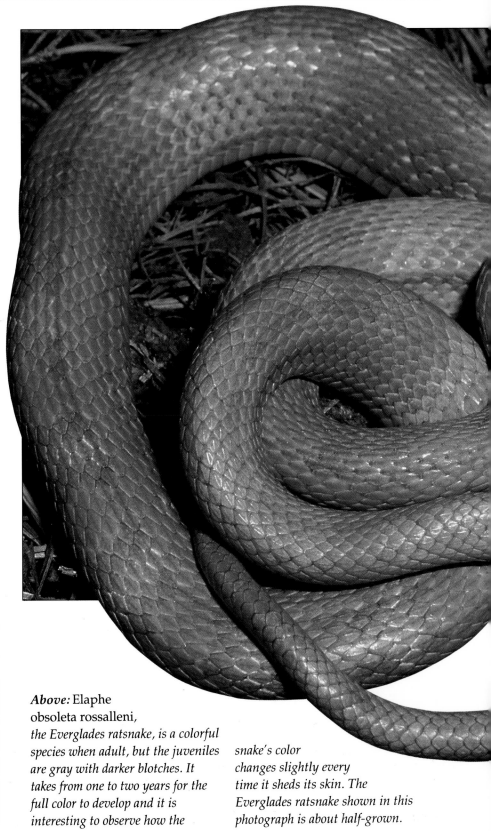

Above: Elaphe obsoleta rossalleni, *the Everglades ratsnake, is a colorful species when adult, but the juveniles are gray with darker blotches. It takes from one to two years for the full color to develop and it is interesting to observe how the* snake's color changes slightly every time it sheds its skin. The Everglades ratsnake shown in this photograph is about half-grown.

Left: This is the "blond" form of the Trans-Pecos ratsnake, Bogertophis subocularis, one of the rarest and most sought after North American ratsnakes. Its large eyes indicate that it is largely nocturnal in habits. It is sometimes listed as Elaphe, its former name.

Below: The Japanese ratsnake, Elaphe climacophora, is one of a number of Asian ratsnakes. Many of them are attractively marked and captive-bred babies are well worth looking out for. Some of them vary slightly in their temperature requirements, but are not difficult to care for.

same basic heating system will suit them all if you provide a range of temperatures as described on page 76. European and North American species can be allowed to cool down over the winter and, in fact, this is often essential if you hope to breed them.

Hibernation

Many individuals of these species stop feeding in the fall or winter, whether they are cooled down or not, because their biological clocks "tell them" that it is time to hibernate. When this happens, the only course of action is to lower the temperature of the enclosure for two or three months and they will then begin feeding well the following spring. Do not allow the tropical species to cool down; they normally continue to feed throughout the year. All species in this group of snakes eat rodents and most learn to accept defrosted mice.

Breeding

Breeding varies according to the species. The European and North American species will breed in the spring and can all be dealt with in the same way. Tropical species breed throughout the year, the female laying several clutches, provided she is given adequate food and is healthy. Having said this, most snakes, even tropical species, are more inclined to breed during the spring and summer and will usually take a "rest" during the winter.

Kingsnakes

Except for the milksnakes (pages 110-111), all the species in the genus *Lampropeltis* are known collectively as kingsnakes and are only found in North America. They are popular because they are attractive, stay relatively small, and are easy to keep and breed. All the species eat mice, although the newly hatched young of some species can prove difficult at first because they feed on lizards in the wild.

Housing

All forms of the common kingsnake require a medium-sized vivarium with a temperature of 68-80°F. A thermal gradient, produced by placing a heat pad under one end of their cage, is the best arrangement. As this species sometimes eats other snakes, including smaller members of its own species, it is safest to house individuals separately. Kingsnakes need somewhere to hide, such as a piece of cork bark or a small box with an entrance hole.

Species of interest

The species with the widest range is the common kingsnake, *Lampropeltis getulus*. This species is divided into a number of different subspecies, of which the most distinctive are the Californian kingsnake, the Mexican black kingsnake, and the speckled kingsnake. The Californian kingsnake occurs in two forms: in one, the white markings are arranged as rings around the body and in the other, they consist of three longitudinal lines from the head to the tail. The Mexican black kingsnake is glossy black all over,

although hatchlings sometimes show traces of markings in the form of small white flecks, especially along their sides. The speckled kingsnake is also black, but has a small white or cream spot on every scale. In addition, there are albino variants of the Californian and speckled kingsnakes.

Other kingsnakes include the prairie kingsnake, *Lampropeltis calligaster*, which is gray or light brown with saddles of darker brown, and a number of "tricolored" kingsnakes, i.e. species that have red, white, and black rings in various arrangements. Of these, the two mountain kingsnakes are perhaps the most attractive. These are the Californian mountain kingsnake, *L. zonata*, and the Arizona mountain kingsnake, *L. pyromelana*. They differ most obviously in the color of their snouts: the Arizona species has a white snout, whereas the Californian has a black one. The latter species is not recommended for beginners because it can be more difficult to feed.

There are several other species of kingsnake from Mexico and adjacent parts of Texas, including the gray-banded kingsnake, *Lampropeltis alterna*, which occurs in a variety of forms, but all are more suited to the specialist. However, the San Luis Potosi kingsnake, *L. mexicana mexicana*, is relatively undemanding. A third Mexican species, *L. ruthveni*, the Queretaro kingsnake, is a tricolored species, but not as brightly colored as the two mountain kingsnakes. None of these species grows quite as large as the common kingsnake and may be kept in a smaller vivarium. They are secretive snakes that require the seclusion of a small hide box and subdued lighting.

Left: The speckled kingsnake, Lampropeltis getulus holbrooki, *is found in parts of eastern North America. It can grow to a length of 48-86in. and is one of the more attractive forms, but has a rather unpredictable temperament. As a precaution, do not handle kingsnakes if you have been handling mice - the smell is often enough to stimulate a feeding reflex and you may get bitten. Like all kingsnakes, this species will adapt well to captivity, preferring a simply arranged enclosure containing a hide box and a water bowl and very little else by way of decoration.*

Left: *The Mexican kingsnake,* Lampropeltis mexicana, *occurs in a variety of forms and subspecies. This one, from San Luis Potosi, is one of the easiest to look after and has a very gentle disposition.*

Below: *Compare this albino form of the speckled kingsnake with the normal form (opposite). Albinos have occurred in several kingsnakes, ratsnakes, and other groups of species and are bred in large numbers for the pet trade. Whether or not you prefer them to the wild version is a matter of personal taste - their care in captivity is identical, whatever their coloration.*

Subspecies of the common kingsnake

Black kingsnake	*Lampropeltis getulus niger*
Blotched kingsnake	*Lampropeltis getulus goini*
Californian kingsnake	*Lampropeltis getulus californiae**
Cape kingsnake	*Lampropeltis getulus nitida*
Chain (or eastern) kingsnake	*Lampropeltis getulus getulus*
Desert kingsnake	*Lampropeltis getulus splendida*
Florida kingsnake	*Lampropeltis getulus floridana*
Mexican black kingsnake	*Lampropeltis getulus nigritus*
Speckled kingsnake	*Lampropeltis getulus holbrooki**

*The Californian kingsnake may be banded or striped, and the Californian kingsnake and the speckled kingsnake also occur as albino variations. Several other variations are also available.

Milksnakes

The milksnake belongs to the same genus as the kingsnakes, *Lampropeltis*, but consists of a single species, *L. triangulum*. Throughout its very large range in North, Central, and South America it shows great variation in colors and markings, and a large number of subspecies are recognized. These snakes are favorites among snake-keepers because they are colorful, easy to keep and breed, and stay relatively small.

Although the North American eastern milksnake, *Lampropeltis triangulum triangulum*, has brown saddles on a gray or buff background, most other milksnakes have red, white, and black markings along the length of the body. These markings may be arranged as complete rings or as saddles. In some specimens, the white rings are replaced by yellow or orange ones and these snakes are sometimes known as "tangerine" phase animals. Adult milksnakes are often not as brightly colored as the hatchlings; many become suffused with black, which may almost obscure the markings altogether. It is believed that the coloration of milksnakes is a ploy to escape predation by mimicking the similarly marked - and poisonous - coral snakes that are found in the same part of the world. North American subspecies grow to about 36in. long, but some of the tropical forms can attain about twice this length.

Of the various subspecies, the most popular ones include the Mexican milksnake, *Lampropeltis triangulum annulata*, the Sinaloan milksnake, *L. t. sinaloae*, the Pueblan milksnake, *L. t. campbelli*, and the Honduran milksnake, *L. t. hondurensis*. The latter is one of the larger subspecies, whereas the other three are smaller forms.

Housing and feeding

Milksnakes are active, often nervous, snakes that resent too much handling. They are best kept in a medium-sized vivarium with somewhere to hide - a wooden or cardboard box with a small entrance hole is ideal - or make a more attractive den using cork bark or a hollow log. Provide a temperature of 68-77°F, preferably using a heat pad. All the subspecies eat rodents, although the hatchlings of some forms are very small and there may be some difficulty in persuading them to eat; in the wild, these forms would normally feed on small lizards for the first few months.

Breeding

Breeding any of the subspecies follows the same pattern as in most colubrid snakes; they mate in the spring after a cool winter period and the females lay 4-12 eggs about seven weeks later. Remove the eggs from the cage and incubate them at about 83°F. They hatch after about 70 days and the hatchlings will require the smallest size of newborn mice for their first few meals. They grow quickly and can reach breeding size within two years.

Below: The Pueblan milksnake, Lampropeltis triangulum campbelli, *is a popular Mexican subspecies and a good choice for beginners. Formerly rare, hatchlings are now produced in large numbers for the pet trade.*

Right: The Sinaloan milksnake, Lampropeltis triangulum sinaloae, *is possibly the most brilliantly colored of the milksnakes, although everyone has their own favorite. This form can be nervous, but hardly ever bites.*

Other North American snakes

A single species of North American snake, *Pituophis melanoleucus*, is known variously as the gopher, bull, or pine snake according to the subspecies in question. This variable species grows to 72in. long, although some forms remain smaller. In all its forms it is a handsome and impressive species. Unfortunately, it can be aggressive, so choose captive specimens with care.

Gopher snakes

The best forms are those from western North America, known as the gopher snakes - the San Diego gopher, *P. m. annectans*, the Sonoran gopher, *P. m. affinis*, and the Great Basin gopher, *P. m. catenifer*. They are all basically yellowish or brown snakes, with a series of darker blotches down their backs. The number and arrangement of the blotches varies according to the subspecies. All these subspecies occur in albino variants and the Great Basin gopher snake also has striped and albino striped varieties

Pine snakes

The two most common forms of pine snake are the northern pine, *P. m. melanoleucus*, and the black pine, *P. m. lodingi*. As its name suggests, the latter is black, whereas the northern pine is white or cream with dark brown or black blotches. Both these subspecies can be rather bad-tempered!

Above: The Sonoran gopher snake, Pituophis melanoleucus affinis, *is smaller and more slender than the bull snake. It is also more docile and is* probably a better choice for the beginner. These snakes often turn up in city parks and backyards, but captive-bred babies adapt to captivity better.

The bull snake

The final subspecies, the bull snake, *P. m. sayi*, is the largest. It is light brown or tan with reddish brown blotches down its back. The temperament of this form varies, although captive-bred specimens are usually quite easily tamed.

Housing, feeding, and breeding

Whichever subspecies you choose, it will require a fairly large vivarium with a temperature of 72-80°F at one end. These snakes eat mice or small rats, which can be stored in a freezer and thawed out before feeding.

Breeding takes place in the spring and the females lay small clutches of 5-10 large eggs about 40 days after mating. At 83°F these hatch out in about 70 days. The hatchlings are relatively large and usually feed on young mice without any problem.

Left: The bull snake, Pituophis melanoleucus sayi, *is among the largest and most impressive of North American snakes. Nervous specimens produce a hiss that can be heard several feet away, but they do not always bite. If possible, buy a hatchling, not an adult.*

Right: The western hognose snake, Heterodon nasicus, *is variable in its coloration, but all forms have plenty of character. It is one of the hardiest North American snakes and will survive long periods without food, especially during the cooler months of the year.*

The hognose snake

The hognose snake is a separate species that comes from the same general area as *Pituophis melanoleucus*. However, it is much smaller, rarely growing to more than a total length of about 24in. Although there are other species, the only one that is suitable for captivity is the western hognose, *Heterodon nasicus*. It will eat mice in captivity, whereas the others are specialist toad-eaters.

The western hognose is heavily built, with a thick body and a short tail. Its most characteristic feature is its snout, which is formed from a sharp-edged scale turned up at the rim. In nature, this enables it to root around in dry soil in search of prey. Hognose snakes frequently hiss loudly and may make mock strikes with the mouth closed. However, they rarely bite unless they are very hungry, in which case they may mistake a finger for a mouse, especially if you have handled a mouse before touching the snake. As their saliva is slightly toxic, do not allow them to chew too strongly, although there is no real danger from a mild bite.

The western hognose requires only a small vivarium and a temperature of about 72-80°F. It likes to burrow, so a thick layer of wood shavings makes an ideal substrate. Some hognose snakes refuse to feed in winter; the best way to deal with this is to remove the heat source and allow them to hibernate for two or three months. When they are warmed up again in the spring, their appetites will return and they will make up for the meals they have missed.

Garter snakes and water snakes

Garter snakes are frequently a beginner's first choice. This is partly because they are often less expensive than other snakes and partly because several species will eat earthworms and pieces of fish, which are usually more freely available than other foods, such as rodents. However, keeping garter snakes healthy in the long-term is not always as easy as you may think. Because of their diet in captivity, many develop vitamin and mineral deficiencies. The only way to avoid or correct this is to sprinkle a good dietary supplement on each food item at every meal. In addition, because their food is not as nourishing as that of other snakes, garter snakes need more frequent feeding; if they are not fed for more than one week, they begin to look thin. Try to feed them every two or three days.

Housing

Garter snakes are diurnal by nature and the best way of keeping them is in a large vivarium with a light bulb or spotlight towards one end. If this is directed onto a flat rock or a piece of dead wood it will create a bright, warm area in which the snakes can bask. Background heating can be provided by means of a low-wattage heat pad, placed under one end of the vivarium and left on at all times. Even though many garter snakes come from damp habitats, keep

Right: The eastern garter snake, Thamnophis sirtalis, *is often sold in pet shops and is the species that introduces more people to snake-keeping than any other snake. It is an active, intelligent snake that makes a good display, provided it is kept in good condition. There are a number of color forms of this species, depending partly on their origin. Garter snakes can be difficult to identify with certainty, but all require similar care and conditions.*

the substrate of the cage dry. Failure to do this will result in sores and blisters developing on the underside of the snakes and these can be difficult to treat effectively.

Species of interest

Of the numerous species and subspecies of garter snake, some make better captives than others. Perhaps the best choice is the checkered garter snake, *Thamnophis marcianus*, which is attractively marked with black squares on a fawn background. The common, or eastern, garter snake, *T. sirtalis*, is one of the most wide-ranging species and is divided into a number of subspecies, all of which adapt well to captivity. These include the red-sided garter snake, *T. sirtalis parietalis*, which is dark in color with prominent red markings on either side of its lighter vertebral stripe, and the Florida garter snake, *T, sirtalis similis*, which is bluish in color. Another attractive species is the plains garter snake, *T. radix*. All these species will adapt quite well to captivity under the conditions described. Other species are not quite as easy to keep.

The ribbon snakes are closely related to garter snakes, but not as easy to look after. They eat mainly frogs and fish and sometimes refuse to eat prey that is not alive.

North American water snakes belong to the genus *Nerodia*. There are several species, some being more colorful than others. The banded water snake, *N. fasciata*, is one of the prettiest and fares quite well in captivity under similar conditions to the garter snakes. However, it will not eat earthworms and must be fed on fish, suitably supplemented with vitamins. You can feed any of the water snakes on whole, small fish or strips of larger fish.

Breeding

If male and female garter snakes or water snakes are kept together, and they are well-fed and in good health, they may well breed. This can take place at almost any time of the year, but is more common in the spring and early summer. The females give birth to live young after a gestation period of several months. The babies are tiny and can number from 5 to 50, depending on the species and the size of the female. Very large females have been known to produce as many as 100 young, but this is exceptional. Remove the youngsters from the adults' cage and rear them separately in small groups. At first, they will only accept small worms or pieces of fish, dusted with a vitamin and mineral supplement as for the adults. During feeding, take care that the young snakes do not swallow one another, as sometimes happens if two baby garter snakes grab the same worm, for example. If regularly fed they will grow quickly and may be large enough to breed after one year.

Left: *The mangrove water snake,* Nerodia fasciata compressicauda, *is rather unusual in that it can live in salty coastal waters. In captivity, you can treat it in exactly the same way as the other members of its family.*

Below: *The checkered garter snake,* Thamnophis marcianus, *is one of the most adaptable species and feeds on a wide range of animal prey, including mice. This makes it rather easier to cater for in captivity and for this reason it is a highly recommended species.*

Turtles

Turtles are perhaps the most appealing of all the reptiles, but bear in mind that unless a very large enclosure is available, only small, freshwater species are suitable for captivity. Turtles have large appetites and produce correspondingly large amounts of waste - in short, they are messy. Large species require frequent water changes, otherwise keeping them becomes a rather obnoxious pastime. However, small species are engaging pets that quickly learn to recognize their owner, especially when food is on offer. Provide a medium-sized aquarium with an area of land for basking. For some species this can consist simply of a piece of flat rock. Depending on the origin of the turtles, maintain the water at the appropriate temperature with a combined aquarium heater/thermostat, and direct a spotlight onto the land area during the day so that the turtles can haul out and bask. Some species require ultraviolet light, and a blacklight is almost essential for rearing baby turtles. Filtration can help to keep the aquarium clean, but undergravel and small internal filters cannot cope with the amount of waste generated. A power filter is therefore essential and the filter medium will need frequent washing or changing.

Feeding

Turtles will eat most types of food, including raw fish and meat. However, an insect diet is the most natural one for them and they only require occasional strips of fish and meat. They also eagerly accept freeze-dried fish food of all kinds, including *Tubifex* and *Daphnia*, but with such large appetites, turtles on a diet of this type can be expensive to maintain. Young turtles require plenty of calcium if their shells are to develop properly. Supply this in the form of cuttlefish bone (as fed to budgerigars), from which they will bite chunks. Freshwater snails are also a good source of calcium, but there is a risk of introducing parasites unless you are sure that they have come from a healthy aquarium.

Species of interest

Red-eared sliders, *Pseudemys scripta elegans*, are the turtles most often seen in pet shops. Unfortunately, the pretty 2in. babies soon grow into greedy 10in. adults, so consider their ultimate needs before buying on impulse. Similarly, the painted turtles, also from North America and often seen for sale as hatchlings, can quickly outgrow a medium-sized aquarium. However, both these species fare well in captivity, provided one or two adult turtles have an aquarium measuring no less than 39x20x20in.

Turtle foods

Many pet stores sell small packs of "dried turtle food," consisting of dried shrimps, insects, etc. These do not constitute a complete diet for turtles and should only be used in an emergency. Pellets or foodsticks specially formulated for reptiles are better, as they contain a balance of all the foodstuffs required by juvenile and adult turtles. Pond pellets are also suitable for larger turtles and more economical, although they are more inclined to foul the water. **All turtles prefer and require fresh food.**

Right: An adult western painted turtle, Chrysemys picta. *In some regions, it may be possible to house these large turtles in an outdoor pond.*

Below: The strange mata-mata turtle, Chelys fimbriata. *Juveniles lose much of their bright coloration as they grow, and the adults can attain a large size.*

Smaller turtle species

If you are looking for a small turtle that will live in a medium-sized aquarium for its entire life, two of the best choices are the North American spotted turtle, *Clemmys guttata*, which only grows to about 4in. long, and the Asian Reeves' turtle, *Chinemys reevesii*, which is similar in size, although not quite as prettily marked. Neither of them require high temperatures and will usually live quite happily at room temperature as long as they have a basking light. The Chinese big-headed turtle, *Chinemys megalocephala*, is sometimes available and about the same size, but requires rather different treatment. It comes from mountain streams and will not thrive under warm conditions. Furthermore, this agile species likes to climb, so place pieces of driftwood or dead branches in the aquarium and install running water if possible, as this is the most natural arrangement for this interesting species.

A selection of other species is available from dealers from time to time. Many of these are tropical species that require heated water, ideally maintained at 68-77°F. Although their diets may vary slightly, most turtles will live under conditions similar to those described. However, do ensure that they are healthy and feeding properly before you buy them, as many of them are in poor condition by the time they arrive at the point of sale. Their eyes should be bright and clear and their limbs should not show signs of physical damage, such as missing claws. Fungus can quickly infect any open wounds. Unless the turtle has been in captivity for any length of time, it should withdraw into its shell when handled. Lethargy is often the first sign that all is not well. Some turtles may harbor bacteria that can cause sickness in humans - always wash your hands thoroughly after handling these reptiles.

Breeding

Only dedicated enthusiasts will succeed in breeding turtles. They require a land area containing a good depth of sand or other substrate in which the female can bury her eggs. The eggs must be incubated at temperatures of 77-86°F and the newly hatched babies need close attention during the first few months of their lives.

Right: The spotted turtle, Clemmys guttata, *is a North American species that is sometimes available from specialist dealers and worth searching for. It eats worms and insects, as well as pieces of fish and pelleted fish food.*

Left and below: Reeves' turtle, Chinemys reevesii, *is a small Asian species that is commonly seen in pet stores. A healthy specimen will quickly adapt to captivity and live for many years without an elaborate set-up.*

Tortoises and box turtles

Shelled reptiles that live on land are usually known as tortoises, although some are also known as box turtles and there is some confusion over what is a tortoise and what is a turtle. Mediterranean tortoises are still seen in pet stores occasionally, although trade in them is now restricted. In addition, specialist reptile dealers sometimes offer North American box turtles and a small selection of tropical tortoises, mainly from Africa.

Housing

Although some tortoises can be housed out of doors during hot weather, they will almost all require an indoor enclosure at some time. An indoor pen can be made from wood and there is no need to fit a lid unless other household pets, such as cats, pose a potential threat. Cover the floor of the pen with bark chippings, straw, or newspaper and provide a dark place for the tortoises to retreat to if they wish. Suspend a powerful spotlight over one end of the pen so that the tortoises can bask and if you include an ultraviolet light, shine it onto the same basking area.

Feeding

Tortoises are almost completely herbivorous and require daily feeding. Offer them a varied diet that includes some fruit, such as tomatoes and bananas, as well as the leaves of lettuce, dandelions, clover, and other wild plant material. Fortify each meal with a vitamin and mineral supplement and give young tortoises additional calcium in the form of ground cuttlefish sprinkled over their food. To discourage the tortoises from selecting just one or two favorite items, chop and mix the food well before giving it to your pets.

Mediterranean tortoises

The Mediterranean tortoises, *Testudo hermanni* and *T. graeca*, can occupy an outdoor enclosure during the summer. This should include a shallow tray of water for the tortoises to drink from and soak in, and also a den, preferably made from weather-resistant

wood, for them to retreat to at night. In some climates it may be necessary to provide shade, so that the tortoises can shelter from the sun during the hottest part of the day. Although the enclosure can be landscaped with rocks and logs, the tortoises will probably eat any plants that you use to decorate it.

As long as they are in good health and have been eating well, Mediterranean tortoises may be allowed to hibernate during the

Right: Hermann's tortoise, Testudo hermanni, *is a Mediterranean species that will often live for many years in semi-confinement outdoors. Take precautions to ensure that it does not become trapped out in the open on frosty nights, however. The exact way* *in which you house it will depend on the climate in your part of the country. Unfortunately, this species has become rare through over-collecting and there are restrictions in force designed to protect it. Do not buy one unless you can care for it properly!*

winter. Place them in a wooden box filled with straw or dead leaves and keep this in a cool place where there is no danger of the temperature falling below 40°F. As the weather warms up in the spring, the hibernating tortoises will gradually become active again and should be removed from their box, given a long soak in tepid water and placed in an indoor enclosure. Keep them here, with artificial heating and lighting, until the danger of sudden spells of cold weather is over and then return them to their outdoor enclosure. However, baby Mediterranean tortoises are not hardy enough to go outside and should be treated in the same way as tropical tortoises.

Above: *The ornate box turtle,* Terrapene ornata, *is just one of several box turtles from North America that can make amusing and responsive pets. You must ensure that they have a good variety of food and protect them from the risk of over-enthusiastic handling by children (and other pets!).*

Tropical tortoises

Tropical species do not hibernate and must be kept warm throughout the year, so housing them is a serious undertaking. Suitable temperatures for them are 77-86°F under the basking light, with a background temperature of at least 68°F. Their diet is similar to that described for the Mediterranean species.

Box turtles

There are three species of box turtle, all in the genus *Terrapene*. They are more omnivorous than other land tortoises, and although they will accept plant material, especially fruits and berries, they also eat insects, worms, and so on. Some will eat canned pet food, but use this with caution as it usually contains too much protein and too little fiber for reptiles.

Box turtles will live outside only during very warm weather. Although they can be allowed to hibernate for short spells, do not subject them to the same low temperatures as the Mediterranean species. Many collectors prefer to treat them as tropical or subtropical species and give them extra warmth throughout the winter so that they remain active.

Box turtles are more agile than other land tortoises and experts at escaping from outside pens. Make sure that the pen is solidly built and cover the top with wire netting if necessary.

Index to species

Page numbers in **bold** indicate major text references and panels. Page numbers in *italics* indicate captions to photographs and illustrations. Other text entries are shown in normal type.

Picture credits

Principal photographer
The majority of the photographs featured in the book have been taken by and are © Chris Mattison

Commissioned photography
Neil Sutherland © Colour Library Books. (Credited by page number and position of the photograph on the page, i.e. (B)Bottom, (T)Top, (C)Center, (BL)Bottom left etc.):

12-13, 16-17, 18-19, 50, 52-53, 54-55, 74, 76-77, 78-79, 104(B), 105(BL).

Additional photographs
The publishers would like to thank the following photographers for providing additional photographs:

David Allison: 48, 72-73(C), 80(BR)

Ideas into Print: 81(TR)

Frank Lane Picture Agency: 43, 85(BR), 88(TR), 89(BL), 98

Marc Staniszewski: 56-57, 69(T), 84(T), 84-85(BC), 85(TR)

W A Tomey: 14, 20, 27, 73(TR), 86-87(T), 87(BL)

Author's acknowledgments
The author would like to thank the following friends and colleagues for their generosity in providing information or for allowing animals in their care to be photographed:

Bob Applegate, John and Linda Bird, Keith Brown (Chester Zoo), Gretchen Davison, Alan Drummond, Dave Garthwaite, Bob and Judy Kenyon (Kenyon Reptile), Jim Knight (Long Sutton Butterfly Farm), Darren Mann, John Pickett, Terry Thatcher, Geoff Trinder, Tom Schultz (San Diego Zoo), Adam and April Wright (Coventry Reptiles).

Publisher's acknowledgments
The publishers would like to thank Tapton Hall of Residence, University of Sheffield for providing excellent facilities for practical photography.